Unmarried
with Children

The Complete Guide
for Unmarried Families

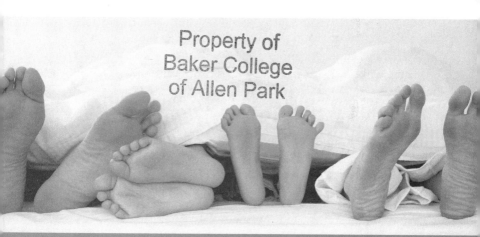

Property of
Baker College
of Allen Park

Brette McWhorter Sember, J.D.,
with Technical Review by Philip S. Hall, Ph.D.

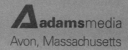
Aadamsmedia
Avon, Massachusetts

Published by
Adams Media, an F+W Publications Company
57 Littlefield Street, Avon, MA 02322. U.S.A.
www.adamsmedia.com

ISBN-10: 1-59869-587-8
ISBN-13: 978-1-59869-587-8

Printed in the United States of America.

J I H G F E D C B A

Library of Congress Cataloging-in-Publication Data
is available from the publisher.

This publication is designed to provide accurate and authoritative information with
regard to the subject matter covered. It is sold with the understanding that the
publisher is not engaged in rendering legal, accounting, or other professional advice.
If legal advice or other expert assistance is required, the services of a competent
professional person should be sought.

  —From a *Declaration of Principles* jointly adopted by a Committee of the
American Bar Association and a Committee of Publishers and Associations

Many of the designations used by manufacturers and sellers to distinguish their
product are claimed as trademarks. Where those designations appear in this book
and Adams Media was aware of a trademark claim, the designations have been
printed with initial capital letters.

This book is available at quantity discounts for bulk purchases.
For information, please call 1-800-289-0963.

Contents

Also by the author:

The Adoption Answer Book

The Complete Gay Divorce

*Gay and Lesbian Medical Rights: How to Protect Yourself,
Your Partner and Your Family*

*Gay and Lesbian Parenting Choices: From Adopting or
Using a Surrogate to Choosing the Perfect Father*

*Gay and Lesbian Rights: A Guide for GLBT
Singles, Couples, and Families*

How to Parent with Your Ex

The Infertility Answer Book

*Your Plus-Size Pregnancy: The Ultimate Guide for
the Full-Figured Expectant Mom*

*Your Practical Pregnancy Planner: Everything You Need to Know about the
Financial and Legal Aspects of Preparing for Your New Baby*

Acknowledgments

Many thanks to my superb agent, Gina Panettieri, friend and partner in my work, and to my editor, Katrina Schroeder, who has been a true pleasure to work with. Phil Hall has been the most excellent of coauthors—knowledgeable and supportive in every way. I would also like to thank the wonderful team at Adams Media, who have supported me every step along the way.

Introduction

This book is meant as a guide and as a support for you, the unmarried parent. Unmarried parents are no longer a quiet minority. More and more couples have children without being married (although some eventually choose to marry later); there is a dramatic increase in the number of single women choosing to become solo parents without a partner; and there are also many gay/lesbian couples choosing to become parents.

You aren't alone. In fact, 1.25 million babies in the United States are born each year outside of traditional marriage. Parents who are raising children outside of a traditional marriage (sometimes together as a couple, sometimes separately) are part of a widespread trend that exists on every social level, even the Hollywood elite: Brad Pitt and Angelina Jolie, Goldie Hawn and Kurt Russell, Susan Sarandon and Tim Robbins, Madonna and her bodyguard (the father of her first child), Jessica Lange and Sam Shepard, and Farah Fawcett and Ryan O'Neal. Hollywood also has its share of single moms having or adopting children alone, such as Calista Flockhart, Camryn Manheim, Mia Farrow, and Sharon Stone. There are also many gay couples raising children outside of marriage, including Rosie and Kelli O'Donnell and Melissa Etheridge and her partner.

The choice you have made to have a child deserves support, encouragement, and recognition. Choosing to become a parent is important, frightening, awe-inspiring, time-consuming, confusing, rewarding, and tiring. Marriage, sexual preference, or living arrangements does not affect anyone's ability to be a good parent. Very little support has been made available to the growing unmarried parent segment of the population, and you're probably aware of the prejudice and stereotypes that some people hold about unmarried parents; it's time for that to change.

You are as much a parent as any other parent out there. This book is written to give you access to the legal and practical information you need to make your job as an unmarried parent easier. Because our society does have a prejudice against people who have children outside of marriage, there are some hoops to jump through in order to deal with the legalities of your situation. This book will help you understand these requirements and guide your decisions about them. Because of the attitude that exists in society, there are problems you may encounter in your daily life as an unmarried parent. In this book you'll find practical solutions to these problems and alternatives for coping with them. Mostly though, this book is designed to be a support for you, to help you remember that what matters is your child and not what other people think.

As with all books that deal with legal issues, it's important to understand that the laws in each state are different and that laws are always changing. To get up-to-the-minute legal advice, it's a good idea to talk to an attorney in your state. This book is meant to be informative, but it cannot give you the personal, individual advice an attorney can, and it is not intended to be a substitute for legal advice.

Each chapter contains "Advocacy Tips." These tips show you ways that laws and perceptions can be changed and offer suggestions for how you can help effect change. In each chapter you will also find a "Life Lesson," a scenario exemplifying real-life situations.

This book is a complete guide for you as you raise your child in a situation that, while it may be considered nontraditional, creates a loving and beautiful family. Raising a child is one of the most important things you will ever do, and my hope is that you'll find all of the information and support you need in this book as you create and enjoy the family of your dreams.

Chapter 1
Making Decisions That Fit Your Life

There are no one-size-fits-all solutions in this world. We are each individuals, and our families are as unique as we are. Because we're all different, we all need to make choices and decisions that fit us and our lifestyle and may not mesh with traditional expectations. As a parent, your first responsibility is to make choices that are best for your family, even if these choices don't seem to be in sync with what the rest of the world expects from you. You are the only one who can make choices for your family, and you have the absolute right to do so in the way that seems best to you.

Parenting Outside Marriage Is Not a Crime

A mere fifty or sixty years ago, having a child outside of marriage was rare and looked down upon (although there were certainly many children conceived outside of marriage then—the difference is many people married because they got pregnant). Today, more and more children are born to parents who are not married. There are parents who purposely decide to conceive children outside of marriage, and there are parents who embrace an unexpected pregnancy when they are not married. In either scenario, becoming a parent is a wonderful thing. A child brings incredible joy and changes your life for the good.

Parents who are not married are able to give their child the things that are most important in life—love, support, financial security, a family, and stability. Marriage is not a predictor of stability; in fact, with half of all marriages ending in divorce, it's far less than a sure thing.

The best parents are those who make decisions that benefit their children, spend time with and offer attention to their children, make children a priority in their lives, and ensure that their child feels loved and cared for. Many married parents do this, but marriage in no way guarantees these things. Any parent, alone or in partnership, can offer these things to his or her child.

Illegitimacy

One of the biggest criticisms aimed at unmarried parents is that by not marrying they don't legitimize their child. This is an old-fashioned concept and one that needs to be rejected. Every child that is born is legitimate. Every child that is born can take his father's name if the parents choose. Every child that is born has a deep and unyielding connection to her parents. Whether a child's parents are married or not has no impact on the child's importance, rights, and status in the world.

Advocacy Tip ▬▬▬▬▬▬▬▬▬▬▬▬▬▬▬▬▬▬▬▬▬▬▬

As a parent, you can help change the mindset about legitimate versus illegitimate children by refusing to allow anyone to refer to your child using that terminology.

Parents' Connection to Each Other

Another argument for why parents should be married is that marriage binds them to each other and ensures they will be around to care for children. Clearly, this isn't true, as the divorce rate shows. Marriage is one way of showing commitment to each other, but there are certainly many more. Many unmarried couples feel that a piece of paper is not as important as their connection to each other. Even if you and your child's other parent are not together as a couple, if you are both involved in the child's life, you have made a commitment to each other as parents. Committing to parent together in a fair and reasonable way is ultimately more important than wedding vows promising to love each other forever.

A Child Is Not a Mistake

Often, people assume that if a woman or a couple has a child outside of marriage, the child's conception was an accident. It's also sometimes assumed that the pregnancy is an embarrassment. When a child is conceived and the mother or both parents decide that they want to raise the child, there is no mistake involved. Regardless of how the conception itself happened, the child is a happy, joyful addition to the lives of the people involved.

Dealing with Traditional Expectations

There are many people who still wholeheartedly believe that first comes love, then comes marriage, then comes a baby in a baby carriage. For some people, this is a natural progression, but for others, it is not. If you are a single parent, gay parent, or part of an unmarried couple, you have become a parent through a different pathway—one that is natural and right for you.

Although you are probably very happy and at peace with the way your life has turned out, others may question you. Often, parents or older relatives are uncomfortable, or you may encounter professionals such as teachers and doctors who simply don't understand your situation. Neighbors may ask uncomfortable questions. Strangers usually will assume you are married if you are an unmarried couple, or divorced if you are a single parent. These assumptions are very automatic in our society.

👫 Life Lessons

Derek and Jennifer have each been divorced. They started living together after they had been dating a year. Soon after, Jennifer became pregnant with their son Austen. Getting married never really occurred to either of them. They had both been in bad marriages and had no desire to repeat the experience. They loved each other and they loved their son. When Austen was a year old, they moved to a larger apartment. Jennifer and Austen met the next-door neighbors. Later that week, Jennifer introduced Derek to them, by saying "and this is my boyfriend Derek." They looked at her oddly. The woman said "Oh, I thought you were married. Whose baby is that?" Jennifer was shocked by such a question. Derek stepped in and explained that Austen was their son together. The neighbors didn't continue the line of questioning and changed the subject. As they got to know the neighbors more, Jennifer became friends with the wife and eventually explained to her about why she and Derek did not marry. Their new friends soon accepted their situation.

When dealing with family, keep in mind that most likely their love for your child will override their objections, or at least help them cope with them. It is a rare grandparent who will reject a grandchild because of the choices of the parents. When dealing with acquaintances and professionals you may meet as you work with your child, remember that most reactions stem from ignorance. Many people simply expect a family to take only one shape and are surprised and unsure how to respond when confronted with something outside their experiences. Remaining sure of yourself and of the choices you have made will help you meet the uninformed inquiries that come your way with dignity and tolerance.

Expectations Are Changing

While there is still a lot of prejudice and ignorance about lifestyles, more and more people are beginning to accept and understand that there are many types of families. There is less of a stigma now than ever before about "unwed mothers," single parents, gay parents, and couples who cohabit without getting married. The gay rights movement has done a lot to change people's perceptions of what makes a family. The Hollywood baby boom has also placed unmarried families front and center in the media's eye, showing even the most conservative Americans that children can be raised in a variety of family settings.

Schools no longer always expect children to have parents that live in the same home or have the same last name. Pediatricians are more supportive of women raising children alone than ever before, and the American Academy of Pediatricians issued a formal statement supporting gay parents. There are many community support organizations designed to assist gay parents or single parents. Probably the last lingering misconception centers around parents who cohabit but who are unmarried. Many people simply do not understand why a committed couple would not marry. This too is slowly changing, as more and more couples choose this option.

Advocacy Tip

Brad Pitt said that he and Angelina Jolie will not marry as long as gay couples are denied the right to do so. One interesting concept that has been proposed in the fight for gay marriage is the suggestion that everyone, regardless of sex, be offered the right to enter into a legal government partnership that would confer all the federal rights of marriage. "Marriage" could then become a religious term and left to individual churches to confer.

Chapter 2
The Legal Rights of Unmarried Mothers

Whether you are a solo parent or part of an unmarried couple, it's important to understand your legal rights as a mother. If you understand your basic legal rights and remedies, you can go forward as a parent armed with all the information that might be needed.

Birth Certificates

If you give birth to your child, you will automatically be listed as the mother on the birth certificate. You have the choice of listing the child's biological father or leaving this part of the form blank. No one can pressure you to complete this line if you choose not to (the one exception is if you are receiving public assistance, the state can require you to name the father in order to continue receiving benefits). If you choose to leave the father's name blank, you may encounter pressure, rudeness, or curious looks from hospital or government employees. Ignore these and remember that this is completely up to you and no one can make this decision for you. In most states the father's name cannot be included on the birth certificate unless he signs an acknowledgment of paternity (see below).

If you adopt your child, the adoption birth certificate will list you as the mother and your partner as the father if your partner is male and if you are both adopting the child.

If you leave the name of the father blank and paternity is later acknowledged or determined by a court (see following sections), a new birth certificate is issued. A new birth certificate also is issued if you and your child's father marry after the birth or if your child is later adopted by your partner.

When a gay mother gives birth to a child, her partner is not the legal parent (except in states where civil unions or marriage have been legalized for gay couples). In this situation, the birth mother should leave the father space blank or write unknown. Then her partner can adopt the child easily, since there is no father to notify or obtain consent from. It's important to note that if a mother knows the name of the biological father of the child, she is supposed to fill it in, so gay couples who did not use a blind insemination process are technically supposed to list the biological father and then obtain his consent to the adoption (see Chapter 6 for more details about adoption). For gay male couples who use a surrogate, both the biological mother's name and father's name appear on the birth certificate, and the surrogate mother then must consent to the adoption by the other partner. A new birth certificate is issued after the adoption.

When a child is adopted by both partners or born to one partner and adopted by the other, after the adoption is complete, one parent is listed in the "mother" section and one parent is listed in the "father" section, although many states are moving to simply use the word "parent" instead of gender-specific terms. Another important point is that parents must list their birth names on the child's birth certificate, so a transgendered person would be required to list his or her original birth name.

Advocacy Tip ▬▬▬▬▬▬▬▬▬▬▬▬▬▬▬▬▬▬▬▬

Ask your state assembly representative to sponsor a change in your state, changing birth certificates to allow spaces with two blanks labeled "parent" as opposed to the traditional forms with spaces for "mother" and "father."

Naming Your Child

When you complete the birth certificate form, you will select your child's name. You can choose to give your child your last name, the father's last name, your partner's last name, or another name, such as a hyphenated combination of the two or any other name you choose. Some states restrict your options and may not allow you to give the baby the father's last name unless he signs the birth certificate. If you name the child's father on the birth certificate, most states require his signature on it—which essentially means he agrees with the name as written. If the father is not named, you do not need his signature or his consent with regard to your child's name.

👫 Life **Lessons**

Andrea and Ahmad were thrilled when their daughter was born. They enjoyed the time they spent in the hospital, holding her, feeding her, and showing her off to friends and family who came to visit. One of the papers in the packet of information they received from the hospital was the birth certificate application. It was at this point that some of their joy diminished. Because they were not married, Ahmad could only be listed on the birth certificate if he acknowledged paternity—something that deeply insulted him. After ranting and raving and scaring one of the nurses, the couple talked to a hospital social worker who explained that Ahmad had to acknowledge paternity because otherwise, women could write in the names of anyone they wanted to for their children's fathers. They had a good laugh when she explained that Bill Gates, Mel Gibson, and the president already had plenty of children and that allowing a mother to simply write in the name of the father wasn't a very good idea unless the father actually agreed. When the parents are married, it is assumed that the husband is the father, although she admitted that might not always be the case. So, Ahmad did sign the acknowledgment and their daughter's birth certificate was issued with both their names on it.

Paternity

Although you and your partner know that he is your baby's father, your state doesn't automatically recognize the relationship that is clear to both of you. When a child is born to unmarried heterosexual parents, the father becomes a legal father if he is listed on the birth certificate, signs an acknowledgment or affirmation of paternity, or if a court issues a determination of paternity.

Acknowledgment of Paternity

An acknowledgment of paternity is a legal document admitting that a man is the father of the child in question and is available at the hospital. This is often used by unmarried couples to legally declare their child as the child of the male partner. You may chafe at the thought of having to jump through these legal hoops, however, having paternity legally established is important so that your child will have the right to receive any survivor or inheritance benefits from his or her father.

Note that because the father acknowledges paternity does not mean that custody, visitation, and child support have been established. These are separate proceedings.

Court Declaration

A court declaration of paternity usually is only necessary when there is some question as to who the father is or if the father is contesting it. A DNA paternity test (DNA samples taken from the father and child are compared using blood or a swab from inside the cheek) will then determine the likelihood of the man in question being the father. Usually these results are quite conclusive (although many people are surprised to realize these tests cannot offer a 100 percent guarantee), but if they are not, the alleged father can insist upon a trial. The court will hear other evidence, such as who the mother had sexual relations with and when it was during her cycle, and then makes a determination of paternity. If the man is found to be the father of the child, a new birth certificate will be issued reflecting this. In some states paternity can be decided if a man acts as if the child is his (this is called "presumptive paternity").

Marriage and Paternity

If a woman is married to a man while pregnant or when the child is born, her husband is the legal father of the child, even if she knows he is not the father. She or the true father can bring a paternity case if DNA shows that the husband is not the father, but unless this step is taken, the husband will remain the legal father.

Not Including the Father

If you do not want the baby's father to have a role in the child's life, you don't have to list him on the birth certificate or notify him in any way about the pregnancy or birth. However, it's important to remember that your child will ask questions, and that most children benefit from having contact with their father if he is known.

The father may decide to register with the state putative father registry—a database that allows men who believe they have fathered a child to record the information with the state. Doing so requires that the father be included in any adoption proceeding should his paternity ever be established.

Legal Authority Without Paternity

Should you choose not to create a legal record of paternity for your child but wish to give authority to a partner or person who is, for all intents and purposes, the child's other parent, there are several things you can do. Use the Consent to Obtain Medical Treatment form (Appendix A) to permit someone other than yourself to get medical care for your child. Consult your child's school and ask what documentation they need to permit the other parent to pick up your child from school and attend parent-teacher conferences and school events. Usually a signed letter will be enough. Chapter 11 about stepparenting offers more information about this.

Talk to an estate planning attorney and create a will in which you designate your partner as the guardian for your child should you die. See Chapter 13 for more information about this.

Custody

If there is no acknowledgment or determination of paternity, the father has no legal right to custody or visitation/access. Once paternity is established, the father has the right to seek custody or visitation/access (child support also becomes an issue once paternity is decided). Even if the parents cohabit, custody has to be legally determined for the father or other parent to have legal rights.

Advocacy Tip

In some ways, custody in our society has become a way to somehow designate the "good" parent and the "bad" parent. If you don't get custody of your child it is sometimes considered to be an indication about your character. This mindset has to change. Custody is simply about arranging and sharing time with a child. It's not a way to punish one parent or champion the other.

The best interest of the child is the determining factor in awarding custody, and there is no preference for mothers over fathers. Courts look at all the circumstances involved, so anything that affects the child is part of the decision.

If you are not a solo parent and you and the other parent have plans for how you want to divide your parenting time, it is still a good idea to get a court order of joint custody/shared parenting time (or sole custody if that is what you want). Doing so will eliminate problems in the future and will give you the peace of mind that all legal matters are taken care of. See Chapters 8, 9, and 11 for information about sharing parenting time between parents.

Custody Terms:

Joint Custody: parents share equal responsibility for the child and make important decisions about the child together.

Sole Custody: one parent is given the ultimate authority with regard to decisions about the child.

Physical or Residential Custody: this refers to the parent the child will primarily live with. Usually one parent is given residential custody, but joint or shared residential custody is a choice.

Visitation: the time a parent is given with a child when he or she does not have residential custody.

Access, Parenting Plan, or Parenting Time: these terms are used by some states instead of the word visitation to describe the time the parents spend with their children.

Informal Agreements

There are many parents who never have custody legally determined. Often if a mother raises a child alone and the father was not named on the birth certificate, there is no reason to determine custody, particularly if the father sees the child infrequently. An informal agreement can work quite well if the father is not interested in being very involved in the child's life. However, if child support is needed, custody does have to be determined first.

﹖ Life Lessons

Lynn and John lived together and were the parents of a five-year-old son, named Ryan. John acknowledged paternity at Ryan's birth. When it came time to go to kindergarten, John took Ryan to register. As John filled out the paperwork, he came to a section that asked for information about Lynn and himself. He filled in their names, address, work phone numbers, and other information. The form asked if the parents were married and he checked no. Then it said, "If no, please indicate which parent has custody." Since Lynn and John had never gone to court to obtain a custody decree, he didn't know how to answer this question. The receptionist at the school told him he had to complete the form.

John took the form home and he and Lynn decided to call a friend who was an attorney. The attorney explained that because they were not married, the school needed to know who had custody of Ryan so they would know who had the right to make decisions for him and where he lived. Lynn and John explained that Ryan lived with both of them and they parent together, just like married parents do. The attorney thought for a bit and said that although their arrangement made perfect sense, it put the school in the position of not knowing which parent Ryan should go with if there was ever a dispute or if they broke up. Lynn and John felt angry and hurt that the fact that they weren't married made it seem as if they were somehow not stable parents. The attorney suggested that one of them file a custody petition in family court seeking joint legal and residential custody and the other file a consent.

Lynn and John thought long and hard before agreeing to do so. They decided that although it seemed wrong that they should have to have a judge say they both had an equal right to parent their son, they wanted to make things in Ryan's life go smoothly. Although they didn't want to get married, they felt that putting on paper what was in fact true—that both of them lived with Ryan and made decisions about his life—was important to do for Ryan's sake. While the case was pending in court, they filled out the school paperwork indicating that the court case was pending, but that Ryan in fact resided with both of them and that they had both agreed to joint legal and residential custody and were waiting for the court to make it official.

After a few months, the family court made a custody order, and Lynn and John were able to complete the paperwork for kindergarten. They later found that this court order came in handy when Ryan registered for summer camp and when

John's employer switched health insurance plans and John needed to include Ryan as a dependent on the insurance.

Child Support

If it is requested, the nonresidential parent is responsible for paying child support to the residential parent. Child support cannot be ordered until paternity is established and custody is determined. If both parents share joint residential custody, the court can still order child support based upon a calculation of each parent's income and expenses.

Benefits and Detriments of Child Support

If you don't want child support, you don't have to ask for it. No one can make you accept it (unless you are receiving public assistance, then your state can require you to file for it so it can be paid to them). Seeking child support can be a mixed bag for some people. If you are a solo mother, know who the father of your child is, and decide you want him to pay child support, you have to understand that he can ask for and obtain visitation and even seek custody of your child as a result of your bringing your arrangement to court. If you are part of an unmarried couple, having a court order child support can sometimes cause bad feelings between parents. However, the only way to ensure that the other parent will support your child now and in the future is to seek child support.

For income tax purposes, child support is not deductible for the parent paying it, nor is it considered income for the parent receiving it. You can choose to handle child support directly between the two of you, or you can have child support paid to the state child support enforcement agency, which will then send the custodial parent the money. Using the agency has a lot of benefits. You and the other parent don't need to talk or argue about when payments were made. There is a clear record. Additionally, the agency will begin enforcement proceedings if payment is not made, and it will also increase child support for cost-of-living increases, when authorized by your state law.

👫 Life **Lessons**

Roy and Ramondo wanted a child together. Roy adopted a one-year-old daughter from China, and the plan was that Ramondo would then adopt her soon after (their state would not allow them to adopt at the same time). Unfortunately, they broke up before Ramondo could complete the adoption process. However, they both felt that Jade was their daughter together. Ramondo continued to spend time with her, although she lived at Roy's home. They planned to raise her as their child together. Ramondo wanted to contribute money to Roy's household to help pay for Jade's expenses, but Roy was too proud to accept it. After offering many times, trying to slip money into Roy's desk, and trying to leave money in Jade's overnight bag, Ramondo realized Roy would never accept money from him. Instead, Ramondo opened an investment account for Jade, as well as a college savings plan in her name and deposited money in both accounts each month. By the time Jade is eighteen, there will be enough money to pay for her college education.

Child Support Rules

If you want to pay support, but the other parent won't accept it, there is nothing you can do to force him or her to accept it. Child support rules apply to married, unmarried, and gay parents. Child support continues until the child reaches age eighteen (in some states it continues through college) or when he or she becomes emancipated—living independently.

Support is usually paid by the parent that does not live with the child, but that is not always the case. Even if the parents cohabit, one can still seek support from the other. Technically, child support is calculated by taking into account both parents' incomes and assigning an amount each is responsible for. In a cohabitation situation, the parent who earns more would probably be the parent asked to pay child support.

Payable child support is calculated as a percent of the nonresidential parent's income. Certain things are deducted from a parent's income (such as taxes and SSI) and other things are added in (certain job benefits, such as a company car), and then a percent is taken for child support.

Child Support Percentages

Most states use the following percentages of income in most cases (it is possible for both parents to agree to opt out of these set percentages) to calculate the basic amount of child support payable by the nonresidential parent:

17 percent for one child

25 percent for two children

29 percent for three children

31 percent for four children

35 percent for five or more children

Even if a parent has no income, he or she is still required to pay the state minimum monthly child support amount.

The nonresidential parent is also usually required to provide the child with health insurance (if available through his or her employer), and to share the costs of medical and dental care, childcare, school, and other expenses. Once child support is paid, the parent receiving it can do anything he or she wishes with the money and need not show it was used to directly support the child.

Advocacy Tip

Many people believe child support laws would be fairer if they required the parent receiving child support to show how it was used for the benefit of the child. Some parents make a point to let the other parent know how child support was used so that he or she can have a sense of its impact on the child's life. Simply respecting that the other parent is making a contribution can go a long way toward keeping discussions about child support civil.

Informal Agreements

There is nothing that prohibits a parent from working out an informal child support agreement with the other parent. If you don't want to go to court, have paternity determined, and have custody decided officially, you can't get child support. However, if you and the other parent are able to work together and have a level of trust, an informal child support arrangement could work for you. Child support is only enforceable, however, if it is ordered by a court. If you don't trust each other, an informal arrangement is unlikely to work. It is also important to remember that although you and the other parent may trust each other today, that doesn't mean you will tomorrow. A court order is the only way to ensure child support will be paid.

Another important thing to remember about informal child support is that if payment is made in a traceable way (such as by check), this can have an impact on the income tax situation of the parent receiving the child support. Court-ordered child support is not income to the person receiving it or deductable for the person paying it. Agreements not entered through a court could have tax implications.

Talking to Your Child about His or Her Parents

Children love their parents because of the role they take in their lives, not because of pieces of paper such as birth certificates or custody decrees. Young children don't need to know the legal details of their situation—all they need to know is that their parent or parents love them. School-age children, tweens, and teens need to know more details as they get older. If you and the other parent are a couple, you may feel it is important to talk about why you never chose to marry and how parenting together has been an important bond in your lives. Single mothers with children who know their fathers will find it necessary to explain at some point why Mom and Dad do not live together. Most children know other children in a similar situation, so this is not difficult to explain, but it is still an important topic and one children will want to discuss. Single mothers whose children do not have another involved parent may have to make a decision about how much information they want to share if the biological father is known. Most children do want to have information about their biological parents, particularly as they become teens and young adults. If a sperm bank was used, it may have a registry that allows both parent and child to register, and if both request it, they can receive information about each other and possibly meet some day.

It's important to remember that what you tell your child about your family's situation is completely up to you. Share what feels right to you, and discuss it in a way that is age appropriate for your child. Sometimes the best way to know what is age appropriate is to listen to the questions your child is asking and use those as your guide.

Chapter 3
The Legal Rights of Unmarried Fathers

There is often a perception that if a man is not married to the mother of his child, he has few rights. This is not the case. A father is as important as a mother and has the same rights to parent as a woman. However, men's rights are more difficult to enforce. When a woman gives birth to a child, there is no question that she is the child's mother (unless she is acting as a surrogate). When it comes to fathers, paternity is not automatic. Father's rights are still extremely important and not that difficult to learn about and enforce.

Birth Certificates

Your child's birth certificate is the record upon which everything else will be based. Because of this, it is easy to feel as if having your name listed on the birth certificate is a crucial point. If you are the baby's father and you and the mother are in agreement about that, having your name listed is a natural step. You will need to sign the certificate to have your name included. Including your name on a birth certificate is a serious step, and in many states it is one step in an admission of paternity (if you're not married there are further steps needed to acknowledge paternity, covered later in this chapter). If you later change your mind and don't believe you are the father, it is difficult to undo, so only sign it if you are sure. Should the mother list your name and you are certain you are the father, you need to approve your name on the certificate and take some further steps to acknowledge paternity (see "Acknowledging Paternity" later in this chapter).

Because the woman gives birth to the child, she has control over the birth certificate application, and if she doesn't want to list your name, she doesn't have to. If this should happen, don't panic. Just because you're not listed on the initial birth certificate, you have not lost any rights. Later in this chapter we'll discuss what steps to take if you were not listed.

If the baby's mother does not list you on the birth certificate, she can either leave it blank or write "unknown," or she could always fill in someone else's name. In most states, the man listed as the father must consent to this, so she can't randomly list anyone she wants.

Advocacy Tip ▬▬▬▬▬▬▬▬▬▬▬▬▬▬▬▬▬▬

In some states, a mother can choose any last name she wants for her child, including that of a man she claims to be the father, even if he has not admitted paternity. It could be disturbing to have a child given your name if you have no legal ties to him or her. If this is the case, you could contact your state elected officials and ask that a law be passed requiring a father to admit to paternity before his name can be used.

Your Child's Name

Choosing a name for your child is one of the first acts you'll do as a parent. Hopefully this is a decision that you and the mother will make together. You can choose any first and middle name for your child that you like—and you must agree, since you both need to sign the birth certificate that lists the names. Additionally, a child's last name is an open choice in many states. Your baby can have your last name, the mother's last name, a combination of the two, or any other last name you choose. Check with an attorney who can verify your state's laws on this topic. Florida, for example, has laws that decide the baby's last name if the parents can't agree, and Montana has a law that states that the child should have the father's last name.

You normally have a few weeks before you need to complete the birth certificate application, so if you want some time to think about or discuss the baby's name, you can take it. You can also change the name you submit on the birth certificate within a certain period of time set by your state, should you change your mind.

Acknowledging Paternity

In most states, if you and the child's mother are not married, you will need to make some sort of legal acknowledgment of paternity (fatherhood) before you will be permitted to sign the birth certificate. This is done to protect you, and to protect the child, so that only men who believe they are fathers become legally involved in the child's life.

Process

Many people assume when they hear the word paternity in a legal setting that it refers to a paternity trial involving DNA testing. If a man and woman agree that he is the father of a baby, no DNA testing is necessary. The man signs a form that is sometimes called a Voluntary Acknowledgment of Paternity. See Appendix A for an example. This form is available at all hospitals and birthing centers in the United States. Once you sign the form, you have a period of time (often sixty days) to rescind it, or change your mind. In only two states is a man unable to complete this form if he is a minor (Kentucky and Wisconsin). This form is legal proof that you have admitted paternity of the child. If there is any doubt in your mind, you should not sign it and should ask for a DNA test.

Proving You Are the Father

If the mother of the child has not listed you on the birth certificate and denies you are the father, but you believe you are, you need to file a case in your local family court. Usually these types of cases are begun by filing a document that is sometimes called a Notification of Filing of Filiation Proceedings. Essentially this means you telling the court and the mother that you believe you are the father and would like the court to decide this matter. The case will proceed like a paternity case filed by the mother (see later in this chapter).

Putative Fathers

If you believe you are the father of a baby being carried by a woman or born to a woman you had relations with, and you would like to have a role in the child's life, you should contact your state putative father registry. This is a database where you can register your name, the mother's name, and the child's date of birth or approximate due date. Registering in this way prevents the woman from putting the baby up for adoption without your consent. If you do nothing and she does not list you on the birth certificate, you have no role in the adoption process and your consent is not required. You can find your state's putative father registry by doing an online search for the name of your state and the words putative father registry or you can find a list at *www.adopting .org/adoptions/national-directory-of-putative-father-registries-fathers-rights-in-adoption-2.html.*

Signing the putative father registry is not the same as going through a paternity proceeding or signing an Acknowledgment of Paternity. Signing the registry simply means you think you could be the father and want to be notified if adoption proceedings are ever begun. It's important to note that the department of social services checks the registry, so if the mother ever goes on public assistance, the department will be able to begin paternity proceedings against you to recoup child support money.

Advocacy Tip

You can find a list of fathers' advocacy organizations online at *www.menstuff.org/resources/resourcefiles/fathers.html.*

Disputing Paternity

If the mother believes you are the father and you disagree, she will need to file a petition in your local family court asking that paternity be determined by the court. This is done by taking DNA samples but also through testimony that describes when the parties had sexual intercourse during her cycle. The DNA results are usually conclusive enough that the case can rest almost entirely on those alone. If a determination of paternity is entered, you then become responsible for child support and can also seek custody or visitation.

‖ Life Lessons

Keith had a one-night stand with Lila. He heard from a friend a few months later that she was pregnant and he was the father. He tried to call her and stop by and see her, and he asked friends to tell her he wanted to help. Although he hadn't planned on being a father, it was a responsibility that he took seriously.

Lila wouldn't talk to him or see him and moved to another city. Keith's mom, who herself had been an unmarried mom, told him he should wait for the baby to be born and hope Lila put him on the birth certificate. She said if Lila didn't, Keith could go to court to be named the father. Several months later, Keith started dating a law student and he eventually told her about the situation with Lila. She told him about the putative father registry and helped him sign up. She told him that it was really important because if Lila put the baby up for adoption, he would have no other way to know.

A few months later, Keith's daughter was born. Lila eventually changed her mind and let Keith have a role in the baby's life, but she admitted she had considered adoption. Keith was glad he entered the registry because he could not imagine life without his beautiful daughter.

Custody

If there is no acknowledgment or determination of paternity, a father has no legal right to custody or visitation/access with the child. This may seem harsh, particularly if it seems quite clear that you are the father. The reason for this rule is that it could be harmful for a child to establish a bond with a man who is later determined not to be the father and who then disappears from the child's life. Once paternity is established, you can seek custody or visitation/access (and child support becomes an issue). Even if both parents cohabit, custody has to be legally determined for the father/other parent to have legal rights.

Custody Terms

Joint Custody: parents share equal responsibility for the child and make important decisions about the child together.

Sole Custody: one parent is given the ultimate authority with regard to decisions about the child.

Physical or Residential Custody: this refers to the parent the child will primarily live with. Usually one parent is given residential custody, but joint or shared residential custody is a choice.

Visitation: the time a parent is given with a child when he or she does not have residential custody.

Access, Parenting Plan, or Parenting Time: these terms are used by some states instead of the word visitation to describe the time the parents spend with their children.

The best interest of the child is the determining factor in awarding custody. There is no preference for mothers over fathers. Courts look at all the circumstances when making a decision, so anything that affects the child is part of the consideration.

If you and the other parent know how you want to divide your parenting time, it is wise to get a court order of joint custody/shared parenting time (or sole custody if that is what you want). This will eliminate problems in the future and will give you the peace of mind that all legal matters are taken care of. See Chapters 8, 9, and 11 for information about sharing parenting time between parents.

Informal Agreements

There are many parents who never have custody legally determined by a court. Often if a mother raises a child on her own and the father was not listed on the birth certificate, there may be no reason to determine custody, especially if the father does not see the child or does so infrequently. It is possible to work out an informal agreement about visitation. As a father, creating this kind of agreement means you see your child only at the mother's discretion. If you have a disagreement, she can keep you away. You have no set rights. However, you can go to court at any time in the child's life and ask for a determination of custody and visitation.

Custody of a Child Up for Adoption

Should the baby's mother decide to place the child for adoption, a man who has registered with the putative father registry and is proven to be the father through paternity testing has an absolute right to custody of the child. The baby cannot be placed for adoption without his permission. The birth father is not an afterthought in an adoption and has legal rights just as the birth mother does. You might be willing to consent to adoption but would like some say in what family the child is placed with; you as the birth father have the right to become involved in this way.

Child Support

If it is requested, the nonresidential parent (male or female) is responsible for paying child support to the residential parent. Child support cannot be ordered until paternity is established and custody is determined. If the parents share joint residential custody together, the court can still order child support based upon a calculation of each parent's income and expenses.

Benefits and Detriments of Child Support

There are many fathers who have negative feelings about child support. Although there is no preference for mothers over fathers when it comes to custody, the fact of the matter is that in the majority of cases, the mother has residential custody, and so most of the time, it is the father who pays child support to the mother. It is absolutely possible for a man to have residential custody and have the woman pay him child support.

When it comes to income tax, child support is not tax deductible for the parent paying it and is not considered income for the parent receiving it. Child support can be paid directly to the mother or through the state child support enforcement agency. Using the state agency might at first seem intrusive, but it has benefits and drawbacks. One large benefit is that there is no arguing with the other parent about what you paid when; there is a clear record of that. However, if you fail to make payments, the state agency will enforce the order. State agencies also increase child support orders for cost-of-living increases when this is permitted by state laws.

Average Child Support

According to the U.S. Census Bureau, the average child support payment made per month in the United States is $350. The median is $280.

While child support may seem like a burden to you, particularly if you did not choose to have a child, it's important to remember that child support serves an important purpose. It is not intended in any way as a punishment, but rather as a benefit for your child. Child support gives you a way to participate financially in your child's life, and knowing that the money you pay provides food, clothing, and shelter for your child can make it seem not so punitive.

If you are a father who has residential custody of your child, the mother will likely have to pay you child support. If you don't want child support, you don't have to ask for it. No one can make you accept it (unless you are receiving public assistance, then your state can require you to file for it so it can be paid to them). You can only seek child support once custody has been established.

Child Support Rules

If you want to pay support, but the other parent won't accept it, there is nothing you can do to force him or her to accept it. Child support rules apply to married, unmarried, adoptive, and gay parents—as long as you are both legal parents of the child, child support applies to you. Child support continues until the child reaches age eighteen (in some states it continues through college) or when he or she becomes emancipated—living independently.

The parent that does not live with the child is usually the one to pay child support. However, if the parents cohabit, one can still seek support from the other. Technically, child support is calculated by taking into account both parents' incomes and assigning an amount each is responsible for. In a cohabitation situation, the parent who earns more would probably be the parent asked to pay child support.

Payable child support is calculated as a percent of the nonresidential parent's income. Certain things are deducted from a parent's income (such as taxes and SSI) and other things are added in (certain job benefits, such as a company car), and then a percent is taken for child support.

Child Support Percentages

Most states use the following percentages of income in most cases (it is possible for parents to agree to opt out of these amounts) to calculate the basic amount of child support payable by the nonresidential parent:

17 percent for one child

25 percent for two children

29 percent for three children

31 percent for four children

35 percent for five or more children

Even if a parent has no income, he or she is responsible for paying the minimum amount of child support set by state law per month.

The nonresidential parent is also usually required to provide the child with health insurance, if available, and to share the costs of medical and dental care, childcare, school, and other expenses.

The parent who receives child support is not required to show that the money was actually used directly for the benefit of the child. He or she can take the money and do anything he or she wants with it. Some parents who pay child support are bothered by this and want to see a tangible output that benefits their child. Should you be in this situation, remember that money you contribute does indirectly benefit the child because it increases the household income, whether or not it seems to be used directly for the child. You do not have the option of withholding child support and instead using the money to directly buy items for the child unless the other parent agrees to this.

Informal Agreements

There is nothing that prohibits a parent from working out an informal child support agreement with the other parent. If you and the other parent are able to work together and have a level of trust, an informal child support arrangement could work for you. However, child support is only enforceable if it is ordered by a court. If you don't trust each other, an informal arrangement is unlikely to work. It is also important to remember that although you and the other parent may trust each other today, that doesn't mean you will tomorrow. Some fathers prefer to have the amount set by a court rather than have ongoing discussions, arguments, and negotiations over an informal amount. However once you get a court order for child support, you can never undo it and go back to an informal agreement. That order will always remain in force and can be enforced at any time.

Talking to Your Child about His or Her Parents

Children love their parents because of the emotional bond between them, not because of legalities such as birth certificates or custody decrees. Young children don't need to know the legal details about their custody situation—all they need to know is that their parent or parents love them and are there to take care of them. School-age children, tweens, and teens are able to learn and understand more details as they become more mature. The rule of thumb is to offer your child enough information to answer his questions. If you do that, you've given him the information he needs at that stage in his life. As he gets older and has more questions, you can offer more information at that point. If you and the other parent are a couple, you may feel it is important to talk about why you never chose to marry and how parenting together has been an important bond in your lives.

If you are a single father and your child lives with you, you'll want to address who the child's mother is and why she is not involved in the child's life. Kids recognize their family is different from others and need to know why. If you are a father whose child lives primarily with the other parent, you may want to talk with your child about how she is an important part of your life. You are a family together. Living arrangements don't change that bond that you share.

It's important to remember that what you tell your child about your family's situation is completely up to you. Share what feels right to you and discuss it in a way that is age appropriate for your child. It's important that both parents talk with their child about their family and offer their own perspectives and feelings. You want to encourage your child to feel proud of his family and to understand how deeply and completely he is loved.

Chapter 4
The Legal Rights of Gay and Lesbian Parents

Gay parents are parents like any others, and although many couples are not allowed to marry or formalize their union due to state laws, the same parenting rules that apply to heterosexual unmarried parents also apply to gay parents. You may be considering adoption as a way to expand your family. A fertility procedure might be another avenue you are considering. Whatever path you are considering, there are a variety of options available.

Adopting Together

If you and your partner want to become parents through adoption, you are probably hoping that you can adopt a child together simultaneously. Unfortunately, in most states, that is not an option and only legally married couples can adopt a child at the same time. However, there are some states that do permit gay couples to adopt together. They are:

- California
- Connecticut
- District of Columbia
- Illinois
- Massachusetts (this is only for gay couples married under Massachusetts law)
- New Jersey
- New Mexico
- New York
- Oregon
- Vermont

If you do not live in one of these states, you and your partner may still be able to adopt a child, but you will need to do it in a two-step process where one parent initially adopts the child and the second then does what is called a "second-parent adoption" (the same concept as a stepparent adoption). If second-parent adoption is not permitted in your state, then only one of you can be a legal parent to your child.

Adoption Process for Couples

If you and your partner would like to adopt as a couple and your state allows this, you will be limited to domestic adoption since most foreign countries with children available will not allow a gay couple to adopt simultaneously (however, you can still adopt internationally in a two-step process). You will need to decide if you would like to adopt a baby or an older child, and whether you want to adopt from a state agency (by adopting a foster child) or through a private agency (the way most babies are available). Another method is to arrange a private adoption, sometimes called parent-facilitated adoption, where you locate a birth mother on your own (usually through advertising or through referrals) and proceed through the adoption without an agency involved.

The adoption process can be lengthy, and there is a lot of paperwork, but you shouldn't let that scare you off. The thing most people worry about is the home study. During a home study, a social worker will come to your home to interview you and anyone you live with (including your partner). You'll need to provide references, medical reports, and go through a criminal background check. It is very important that you use an attorney who is experienced in adoption throughout the process because if the adoption is done wrong it is invalid.

If you are adopting simultaneously as a couple, your relationship is out in the open and you have nothing to hide. If you are adopting in a two-step process where one parent adopts first and the other later, it is possible to conceal the fact that you are gay in the first adoption.

Adopting Separately

Many gay and lesbian people choose to adopt children on their own or adopt in a two-part process with their partner. The only state that does not permit adoptions by gay people is Florida. The key thing to remember when adopting alone or separately is that your sexual orientation is not legally relevant and most social workers who do home studies and agencies that interview you will not ask you if you are gay. There's a "don't ask, don't tell" policy in place most of the time. However, if someone does ask if you are gay, you should not lie, as you don't want to create any cause for the adoption not to go through, and lies or fraud will definitely cause a problem.

A study in Adoption Quarterly found that 63 percent of public and private adoption agencies accept adoption applications from gay and lesbian singles or couples. Agencies that identify themselves as fundamentalist Christian or Catholic were least likely to accept applications from openly gay people.

Adopting Alone

If you are single and want to adopt on your own, you should not encounter problems. Many single people, gay or straight, have adopted, so single adoption is fairly commonplace. As a single person, you can adopt domestically or internationally. When adopting alone, it is important to demonstrate to the social worker that you have a support system in place to help you raise your child. You need to think about who can help you, who can back you up, and who can help provide role models.

Second-Parent Adoption

Second-parent adoption is a two-part process where one person goes through an initial adoption to bring the child into the family. The other parent then adopts the child through a modified process that is not as difficult. You can also do a second-parent adoption if your partner has a biological or adoptive child from a previous relationship. If there is another legal parent (such as your partner's former spouse) he or she must consent to the adoption.

Some states have laws that clearly permit second-parent adoption for straight and same-sex couples. These include:

- California

- Connecticut

- District of Columbia

- Illinois

- Massachusetts

- New Jersey

- New York

- Pennsylvania

- Vermont

There are other states that have permitted second-parent adoptions by same-sex couples, but they have no clearly enunciated rule. These include:

- Alabama
- Alaska
- Delaware
- Georgia
- Hawaii
- Indiana
- Iowa
- Louisiana
- Maryland
- Michigan
- Minnesota
- Nevada
- New Hampshire
- New Mexico
- Ohio
- Oregon
- Rhode Island
- Texas
- Washington

Second-Parent Adoption Procedure

In order to do a second-parent adoption, the legal parent must consent, and in some states, the first parent actually has to readopt the child with the partner in the procedure. Home studies are sometimes waived when a second-parent adoption is being done, and other times they are required. If a home study is required, it is usually nothing to worry about and is just another part of the procedure. The court procedure for a second-parent adoption is streamlined as well. Since you and your partner are in agreement, there are no surprises possible with a birth mother changing her mind. Once the adoption is complete, you'll be issued a new birth certificate for your child that lists both of you as parents.

Advocacy Tip

For help, support, and advocacy opportunities for gay parents, contact the Human Rights Campaign, *www.hrc.org.*

Custody

Just like any couple, gay parents may live apart while still in the relationship, live together, or live separately after a breakup. There is no "correct" living arrangement, and anything that works for you and your child is fine.

If you and your partner are both legal parents of your child, but do not cohabitate, you may want to get a formal declaration of custody from family court so that there can be no question as to where your child should live or how you will share your parenting time. A custody order may be necessary to deal with your child's school procedures, such as who can pick a child up from school.

👫 Life Lessons

Micheala and Toni had been together for several years and decided they wanted to start a family. After considering all the options, they chose to apply to adopt a child from China. After interviewing several international adoption agencies, they found one they were comfortable with. They began the application process with Toni as the person applying for the adoption. A home study was done, and Toni had to complete a lot of paperwork and pay numerous fees. Almost a year later, Toni and Michaela flew to China to bring home their baby daughter. Because Toni was the only legal parent, she completed necessary paperwork to let medical care providers know that Michaela had the authority to make decisions about the baby. Michaela couldn't help but feel somewhat insulted that this was necessary, but to protect their family, she agreed it was important. After settling into their new roles as parents, Michaela began a second-parent adoption procedure, which is allowed in their state. Another home study had to be done, and Michaela had to go through a background check, but eventually the adoption was approved. On a sunny spring morning, Toni and Michaela went to the courthouse and the judge signed papers officially making them parents together. They received a new birth certificate in the mail. At last, they were a family.

However, if you and your partner, or ex-partner, don't want a court involved in your lives, no one can force you to do so. As long as you are in agreement about your child and how you share time with him or her, you don't need a piece of paper sanctioning your lives. Many gay couples feel particularly averse to this because their state would not allow them to recognize their union and yet it wants to get involved when they break up.

If you do end up in court with a contested custody case, it makes no difference to the court that you are gay and it also makes absolutely no difference who adopted the child first or whether one of you is the biological parent. If you are both legal parents, you both have rights to the child. Custody will be determined based upon what is in the best interest of the child by looking at all of the circumstances involved.

Child Support

If you and your partner or ex are both legal parents of your child, you can seek court-ordered child support from your local family court. For information about child support rates, see Chapter 2 or 3.

You and your child's other parent are free to make arrangements for child support on your own, but you need to remember that these types of arrangements are not enforceable by the courts. Additionally, traceable (such as by check) payments can have an impact on your tax situation in contrast to child support paid through a formal child support order.

Stepparenting

If your partner has a child from another relationship and the child's other parent is involved in the child's life, you can't adopt the child and can never have a legal bond. Nonetheless, stepparents play an important role in the life of a child. Even if you aren't permitted to have a legally recognizable relationship with the child, you can still share a close bond and, in the child's eyes, fill an important parental role.

Stepparenting Through Your Relationship

Although you may not have a legal bond with your stepchild, you probably do fill the role of a parent in your child's life. There is a basic conflict between your real, day-to-day role and your role in the eyes of schools, medical care providers, and governmental agencies. Because you aren't a legal parent, you can only have authority over your stepchild if your partner gives you that authority. Therefore, it is very important that your partner create the written documents that are discussed in Chapter 12, such as school and medical authorizations, which will give you the right to make decisions for, and essentially act as a parent toward your child in official settings.

How you and your partner parent your child may be dependent on the child's situation. If the child has another legal parent who is involved in the child's life, the two legal parents need to find a way to jointly make decisions and share time. As a stepparent, you have an important role, but you sometimes may have to take a backseat to the authority of the two parents. It is possible for all three of you to work together for what is best for the child, although this might require setting aside your differences with each other.

However, if you and your partner are the child's only parents, and you are unable to become a legal parent because your state won't allow you to adopt, you are in a different situation. You are the child's parent in all ways except in the technical view of the law. You and your partner work together to parent your child and make decisions.

Stepparents after a Breakup

Should you and your partner decide not to continue your relationship, you may wish to continue your relationship with your stepchild. The best way to do this is to talk with your ex and help him or her understand that continuing the relationship is healthy for the child. If you aren't able to work anything out, there is little recourse in a court. Although some courts have granted stepparents visitation or custody, it is usually only in a situation where the stepparent assumes a primary parental role over a period of time.

Obtaining Custody of Your Child from a Heterosexual Marriage

If you were married and had a child and have divorced or plan to, you may be concerned about how a court will treat you and whether being gay will have any impact on your chances for custody or visitation. Being gay has absolutely no effect on your ability to obtain custody. If you have found a partner, this should have no impact on your case either. Are there some older judges who harbor prejudice? Certainly, but the case law in most states is completely clear: custody is determined based upon what is in the best interest of the child, and being gay has no negative impact on that.

Assisted Conception or Surrogacy

There is a long list of ways you can become a parent in this day and age. If you would like to have a child on your own or with your partner and are not considering adoption, there are assisted fertility methods available.

Insemination

There are several choices available to lesbians when it comes to insemination.

- **You may wish to go to a sperm bank and choose an anonymous donor.** A sperm bank tests all donors for diseases, carefully maintains the donations, and offers you detailed background and medical information about the donors. You can purchase several vials if you would like to have children who are siblings. Some sperm banks also maintain registries that allow children to contact their biological fathers if both parties agree.

■ **You can obtain sperm through a known donor, such as a friend or a relative of your partner's.** Make sure you look for a sperm bank that is accredited by the American Association of Tissue Banks and that follows the guidelines recommended by the American Society of Reproductive Medicine. Choosing a known donor allows you to choose someone you know well, allows more privacy, and may allow the child to have an ongoing relationship with the donor if that's what all involved would like.

Once you've decided how you would like to obtain sperm, you need to select an insemination method. You may choose to have a physician perform the insemination or you may choose to do a home insemination.

No matter what kind of insemination you plan, you need to pay attention to the legal details. If you use a sperm bank, they handle consents from the donor, and you will also have to sign an agreement. If you use a known donor, you need to work with a reproductive rights attorney who will make sure the legal consents are executed properly so that everyone involved is protected.

Advocacy Tip

The FDA bans gay men from being anonymous sperm donors because of the risk of HIV. Because of this, many doctors doing insemination from private donors now refuse to do so if the donor admits to being gay. In a time when there is advanced HIV testing available, this kind of ban is discriminatory. It's a good idea to talk with your doctor in advance about the clinic's or office's policy on this if you are interested in using a gay man as a donor.

When you use insemination to have a child, the woman giving birth is the legal mother. If your state allows gay marriage, and you have gotten married, the mother's partner will also be a legal parent. In all other instances, the partner will need to do a second-parent adoption (if permitted in your state) to become a legal parent.

Surrogacy

Surrogacy is an option that allows a gay man or gay couple to parent a child by insemination of a surrogate mother. Some couples know which partner they would like to be the biological father, whereas others provide a mix of sperm for the insemination so that they don't know.

Advocacy Tip

Fertility clinics cannot discriminate against people because of their color or a disability, yet there is no federal law preventing discrimination based on sexual orientation. Currently there is a California case making its way through the courts about discrimination against a lesbian by a fertility clinic. Stopping this kind of discrimination is an important step in making fertility treatments available to all people.

There are two types of surrogacy. In traditional surrogacy, the surrogate's own eggs are used. In gestational surrogacy, eggs are provided by a donor and do not come from the woman carrying the baby. Gestational surrogacy provides an opportunity to use eggs provided by a relative of the partner who is not contributing sperm so that the baby is related to both partners; however, this creates another step and reduces the odds of achieving a pregnancy.

The laws involving surrogacy are complicated and vary greatly from state to state. The following states have made it a crime to pay for surrogacy (but have not outlawed unpaid surrogacy):

- Michigan

- New Mexico

- New York

- Washington

Sixteen states have laws that make surrogacy contracts unenforceable, which means if there is a dispute and you go to court, the court will not enforce the terms of the agreement. There are no laws that ban you from using surrogacy.

California is the most surrogacy-friendly state, with a court process in place for the intended parents to become legal parents before the child is even born. Illinois is another surrogacy-friendly state. In other states, the biological father is the legal father upon the birth. If he has a partner, that partner can become a legal parent by using a second-parent adoption procedure if one is available in that state.

Many people using surrogacy do so through surrogacy programs run by fertility clinics. The clinics vet all surrogates and there is a lot of backup. Other people choose to locate surrogates on their own and enter into a private arrangement with no one else involved. No matter how you go about locating a surrogate, it is essential that you have a solid agreement in place and that all parties involved undergo counseling and evaluation before creating a pregnancy.

Naming Your Child

When you become a parent, it may be important to you that your child has a last name that links him or her to both parents. If you and your partner adopt together, you will have no problem selecting a combination name or name you both share. If you have to use a second-parent adoption after an initial adoption or fertility procedure, you can wait and change the child's last name to reflect both names at that point.

If you live in a state that requires you to use a parent's last name for the child but does not allow a second-parent adoption, you may feel frustrated that you cannot give your child your partner's name or a combination of both names. One option is to change your own name, or you and your partner to both change your names. You might choose one last name for the family or choose a hyphenated name. Once you've done this, you can adopt or have a child born into the family with that name, or change the last names of any existing children.

Dealing with Expanded Families

When you create a family using modern family-building techniques, such as adoption, insemination, or surrogacy, your child has expanded ties. Whether you want to include birth mothers, donors, or surrogates in your lives is a choice only you can make, but many families in these situations do. With the growth of open adoption, more and more children have contact and bonds with the people who provided their genetic material.

There are a lot of different ways to plan future interaction with your child's biological parents or donors. You might send updates and photos by e-mail or mail. If a donor or surrogate is a close friend or family member, you might designate that person as a special aunt, uncle, or godparent to the child and include him or her in birthday celebrations and important moments.

Some gay families partner with gay families of the opposite sex and create a large extended family so that their children will have companionship and male and female role models. Gay singles often do the same thing with other single gay parents.

Your child's family is what you make it. You can invite special people to share a role in your child's life to whatever extent you are comfortable with. What matters most to your child is that loving, caring, adults surround him or her. The biology and legalities of it are things that can be explained in time.

Chapter 5

The Rights of Children of Unmarried Parents

When we think about parenting, we often focus on the parents' rights, but children have rights as well. Sometimes the interests and rights of children conflict with or do not completely align with the rights of the parents, so it is important to keep in mind what is best for your child, even if it might not be exactly what is right for you. Being a family is about compromise. Not only do you need to compromise with your partner, but also with your child's needs.

Contact with Both Parents

Whenever possible, it is best for children to have relationships and regular contact with both parents. This is not to say that children raised by single parents are disadvantaged—it is certainly possible to grow up healthy and well adjusted when you are raised by only one parent. However, in cases where there is another parent, children deserve to be allowed to develop a relationship with that parent. The fact that the child's parents are not married in no way affects the child's right to have contact with both parents.

There are good reasons why a parent might be out of the picture, and certainly if a biological parent wants to remain only a donor or birth parent, that should be respected. But if both parents are available and willing to be part of a child's life, including them usually creates a full and rich experience for the child.

If you and the other parent have had a nasty breakup or were never a couple, allowing that parent access to your child can be one of the most difficult things you will ever do. But putting aside your own situation is important because your child can and needs to have an independent relationship with that parent. Your child's rights have to take precedence over your own discomfort. In most cases, if that person was good enough to conceive a child with, he or she is good enough to be a parent to the child that resulted.

When couples go to court about custody, decisions are made based on the best interests of the child, not on what the parents want. It is easy to think about parenting time as what you want or need, when in fact, the primary consideration has to be what your child needs.

Knowledge about Biological Parents

If you adopted your child or used a donor or surrogate, your child is going to want to know where he came from, how he was born, and how you became his parent. There are many ways to handle this quest for knowledge from your child.

Most parents offer explanations that are age appropriate. As the child grows older, he or she can learn more details. If you participated in an open adoption or used a known donor, you can share what information you do have about that donor or biological parent with your child as you feel comfortable, and as your child is able to understand it.

When your child becomes an adult, he or she has the right to pursue more information about his or her biological parent(s), whether you agree or not. Most experts believe that it is best if you support these efforts, even if you feel conflicted about them. As your child's emotional parent, your position is not in jeopardy.

Child Support

While it may seem as if child support is paid for the benefit of the child's residential parent, in fact, child support is meant to benefit the child and is a right that belongs to a child. Although there are no requirements as to how child support payments must be used, they are intended to ensure the child has a good standard of living.

Child support also can include provisions for payment for education, school expenses, health care, health insurance, and other personal expenses directly tied to the child (such as lessons or school clothes). It is not uncommon for a parent to take out a life insurance policy with the child as beneficiary as insurance for the child support. This serves as backup. Should the parent die before the child becomes an adult, the money from the policy can be used to support the child instead of child support money.

What is important to remember is that both parents have an obligation to financially support their child, and this is an obligation you should discuss and share when possible. The obligation to support a child ends when he or she becomes emancipated (lives independently on his own).

Legal Representation

If you and your child's other parent ever should go to court over custody, you're both entitled to legal representation. Your child is too. Whenever a case involving custody or visitation is filed, your child has the right to have an attorney, appointed by the court and paid for by the state, who will represent the child's interests. The parents have no say in who this attorney is; however, most states require that these attorneys undergo special training and be appointed to a panel that the judge then chooses a name from.

This attorney is usually called a law guardian or guardian ad litem. He or she has a special role in the case. Unlike attorneys for the parents, who argue for whatever their clients want, a guardian makes his or her own determination about what is best for the child. If the child is mature enough to have a reasoned opinion, the guardian usually must consider it, but is not always required to act upon it.

Advocacy Tip

If you go to court and a guardian is not appointed, most of the time you can simply ask the court to do so. Most courts do not want to appear to be neglecting the interests of the child by denying him or her representation.

In some jurisdictions, guardians make an independent report to the court about their findings and offer a recommendation about how they think the case should be resolved. In other jurisdictions, the guardian is simply asked to take a position and be able support it by questioning witnesses and presenting evidence at the trial. A guardian does a lot of footwork in the case and often visits both homes, personally interviews the parents and child, and may also talk to teachers and therapists. Once a guardian is appointed, he or she must agree to any proposed settlement the parents are considering.

If the parents cannot afford attorneys for themselves, they can represent themselves (family court is very user friendly). In some situations, a parent with income at or below the poverty line may be assigned a state-paid attorney.

Benefits If One Parent Is Deceased

There are a wide variety of benefits that children of a deceased legal parent may be entitled to. These include retirement benefits and military pensions. Generally these types of policies and programs require that the child be a legal child of the deceased, however, sometimes if a child is designated as a legal child for the purposes of Social Security survivor benefits (see later in this section for more information), this designation will be accepted by the policy or program in question. There is no way to independently designate a child that is not your legal child to be a recipient for these kinds of benefits.

Children are entitled to receive Social Security benefits from a deceased parent until the child reaches age eighteen. Additionally, a child of a disabled parent is entitled to receive Social Security disability payments. Under Social Security law, you must prove that the parent was living in the same home as the child, or was providing or spending money for the support of the child. Interestingly, there are several ways a person is considered a legal parent of a child for the purposes of Social Security law:

- a court order that found the deceased to be the child's parent

- written acknowledgment of parentage by the deceased during his lifetime (such as a notarized letter from the deceased stating that he is the father of the child)

- DNA paternity/maternity test

- strong evidence that the deceased widely acknowledged the child as his own during his lifetime (this can include photographs, written cards or letters, school records, tax records, baptismal records, insurance records, and testimony from other people)

Note that the Social Security Department regulations were written for the determination of paternity and are not written so as to allow a woman to be declared a parent, although there is the possibility that this could be challenged.

Inheritance

Children have a right to inherit from a legal parent upon the death of that parent. Although having a will is an important step for a parent, each state has laws (called intestacy laws) that govern what happens if a parent does not have a will. A person who dies without a will is described as dying intestate. When a person dies intestate, his or her estate is usually divided among the spouse (if there is one) and any surviving children. Someone is considered a child for the purpose of these laws only if the person who died is that person's legal parent. It does not matter if they are biologically related. It is possible to disinherit a child by specifically leaving him or her nothing in a will.

If your child has a stepparent who functions as a parent but is unable to adopt the child, the stepparent can include the child in his or her will. However, if the will does not specifically provide for the child, that child will get nothing. Additionally, a biological parent or donor who has signed away all rights to a child can leave an inheritance to that child in a will, but if it is not included in the will, that child would get nothing under state laws.

Most states have laws that provide an inheritance to children born into or adopted into the family after the will was written. These are called after-born children, and the inheritance for the other children in the will is usually split among all the children alive at the time of the death of the parent.

ŤŤ Life Lessons

Amy and Shane had a two-year-old son, Tyler, together. They lived together as a family. When Tyler was born, Shane was deployed in Iraq and was not there for the birth. When Shane returned from active duty, Amy intended to have him sign the paperwork making him the legally recognized father. However, she never got around to it—there seemed to be so many other things that were important. Sadly, Shane was killed in a car accident. Because Shane did not have a will and because he and Amy were not married, she was not entitled to his estate. Shane had already been cremated when Amy discovered that she would need to somehow prove paternity to the court handling the administration of his estate. A DNA test was no longer possible. Amy also learned Tyler would be entitled to Social Security benefits, as well as a military benefit. She had to go through a lengthy process of providing photographs, getting testimony from family, and completing affidavits to prove Tyler was in fact Shane's son and was entitled to his estate and benefits.

Chapter 6
Adoption by Unmarried Parents

*An unmarried couple can adopt a child together and become parents.
This chapter will discuss adoption by unmarried heterosexual couples.
The information in this chapter is different from the same-sex adoption
chapter in some ways, but the laws often work in the same way in these two
situations.*

Your Right to Adopt

In recent years, the rights of unmarried persons to adopt have increased.
Twenty or thirty years ago, it was unheard of for an adoption to be granted
to a single or unmarried parent. Today that is changing radically.

Whether you are adopting alone or plan to create a family with your
partner, adoption is an option that has become easier than in the past.
There are several types of adoption available to you.

Domestic Private Agency

If you choose to adopt a U.S. child through a private adoption agency,
you will likely have a long wait. Using this kind of adoption, you can
raise your child from birth on, and be the only parent(s) he ever knows.
Every state permits single people to adopt; however, you will need to
find out what the requirements are of the specific agencies you are
interested in. Most agencies will work with single or unmarried parents,
but there are some that will not. It is important to ask up front about
their policies so that you will not be disappointed later on. The adoption
agency handles all of the paperwork and works with the birth mother in
case there are any bumps in the road.

Your choice of agency will be key. When a birth mother decides to
place her baby for adoption, she works with one agency. There is no
database of babies available that any agency can access. So, it is important
to work with an agency that has a good reputation and that has lots of
babies to place.

Advocacy Tip

No matter what type of adoption you are considering, hiring
an experienced adoption attorney is the best way to protect
yourself throughout the process and to ensure that the
adoption will go smoothly. Do not ever think you can do an

adoption on your own or that you can trust the agency to handle all the legal matters.

Because the entire process takes place in the United States, the process is somewhat easier to understand and there is no foreign travel involved. You may be able to meet and have contact with the birth parents. If you aren't comfortable with the birth parents, you can wait for another baby. Whether you are interested in an open adoption (where the birth mother's identity is not a secret) is a matter of choice. However, most birth mothers do have a specific preference about what kind of adoption they are interested in. If she is not interested in an open adoption, it's not going to be an option for you with that birth mother.

Domestic Public (State) Agency

State-run agencies have many children available for adoption, most of whom are placed in foster care because of neglect or abuse. Because being freed for adoption from foster care is a lengthy process, most of these children are toddlers or older children. Unfortunately, the older the child, the less likely that he or she will ever be placed with a family. If you want to adopt from a state agency, there are many, many children available this very minute.

State agency adoptions are the least expensive of all types of adoption. If you are interested, you may be able to adopt a sibling group—these children are very difficult to place and there is great need of parents willing to adopt a family of children. Children who come from public agencies are often minorities (only 38 percent of public agency adoptees are white) and many have developmental delays or other special needs (about two-thirds are characterized as special needs).

Children with Special Needs

There are several types of funding available for parents who adopt children with special needs. Because these children need additional care, there is Title IV-E funding available from the federal government. Additionally, state agencies will enter into an adoption assistance agreement, which is a contract between the parents and the state agency that specifies the payments the state will make to the parents. If you are considering adopting a child with special needs, ask for this kind of funding, and make sure contracts are in place before the adoption is finalized.

Because the children from state agencies tend to be older, they may have established bonds with their biological families, and although the adoption severs the legal bonds, they may remain attached emotionally (even children who were abused or neglected by their parents continue to have an emotional bond with the parents). Keep in mind, though, that it is very possible for a child to continue to have a bond with a biological parent while bonding with and loving an adoptive parent. Single parents and unmarried couples are welcomed by public agencies, and you almost never encounter prejudice about your marital status.

Nonagency Adoption

A nonagency adoption is also called a parent-facilitated adoption. You locate a birth mother on your own or with the help of an adoption facilitator (check with your attorney about facilitators—they are not licensed in many states) or adoption attorney. Because single-parent adoption is permitted in every state, you have no legal barriers. However, some biological mothers want to place their babies with a married couple, so it may take a bit of work to locate a birth mother willing to work with a single or unmarried parent.

Working without an agency is a bit like working without a net. Because of this, many parents who find a birth mother on their own then turn to an agency to help them process the adoption and work with everyone involved throughout the process.

International Adoption

International adoption is very newsworthy, with many single celebrities going overseas to adopt children in recent years. Despite this, international adoption is really the least friendly type of adoption for single or unmarried parents. Some countries simply will not permit it, while others have placed limits on the numbers of single parents adopting from their country. To find out what countries are currently allowing single-parent adoptions, check with a reputable agency that handles international adoptions. Countries that have allowed single-parent adoptions include Brazil, Russia, India, El Salvador, Honduras, Ethiopia, Peru, Bolivia, China, Columbia, Guatemala, Panama, Vietnam, and Kazakhstan. Although China permitted single-parent adoption in the past, it has now banned it. This could change in the future, though, so it is important to get updated information from a good agency.

An international adoption is more complicated legally than a domestic adoption. You work with a U.S. agency that works with an overseas agency to find a child. You will likely need to travel to your child's country and go through a legal process there—which may seem very unfamiliar compared with U.S. legal processes. You must work with the U.S. Citizen and Immigration Services to get permission to bring your child into the United States, and then, in most cases, you will need to go through a U.S. adoption procedure in your state. Your adoption agency will help you through all of the paperwork and will provide translators and guides in your child's country of origin. Children adopted internationally rarely arrive in the United States before they are older babies or toddlers.

Adopting a child from overseas allows you to expand your family's cultural ties. However, you may not receive a lot of information about your child's family history or medical background. Additionally, it may be difficult or impossible for your child to ever locate or know the identity of his or her birth parents. There are some situations where you can learn about the child's birth family and stay in touch with them, but because many children are anonymously placed in (or even left on the steps of) orphanages, in most cases, family heritage is a mystery.

The Adoption Process

The most important thing to remember about adoption is that while it is a life-changing, emotional process, it is also first and foremost a legal process. Because of this, there are forms, waiting periods, and processing times to deal with. Take things one step at a time, and you will make it through the process no matter how lengthy it might seem to you at times. There are plenty of children available for adoption, so you can feel confident that you will become a parent.

Choosing an Adoption Agency

If you choose to work with an agency to adopt, you should interview a few and select the one that you are most comfortable with and that seems to be a good fit. Adoption is expensive. You want to be sure to choose an agency that will give you what you're paying for. Agencies can be either for-profit or nonprofit, but all charge fees. Agencies can be religious or nonsectarian, but it is important to know that most religious-based agencies do not require adoptive parents to be members of that religion.

The best way to locate an agency is by word of mouth, through adoption support groups or people you know who have used an agency successfully. Once you have a few agencies to consider, make an initial phone call and request information by mail. You also need to check their Web site. It does not hurt to do a search to see what people are saying about them in adoption chat rooms online, such as *www.adoption.org/ adopt/adoption-chat-rooms.php*.

Don't sign up with any agency before you've had time to ask questions, compare it to others, and think about the decision. Find out when their next informational meeting for prospective parents is and go to it. Ask questions and be observant. Go up at the end of the meeting and talk to the representatives from the agency. Then schedule an interview so you can get to know the agency and they can get to know you.

Get information about all fees the agency charges. There are normally fees to cover the home study, application, birth mother's expenses (if it is a domestic private adoption), and other costs. The agency should clearly break out these separate amounts for you to see. Be wary of any agency that lumps total costs together and will not provide a breakdown.

Other questions to ask agencies you are seriously considering include:

- Are you licensed in this state?

- How long have you been in business?

- Can you provide references?

- Do you handle domestic or international adoptions? If both, which do you place more often?

- Can you place children from other states?

- Do you have religious restrictions?

- What other guidelines or restrictions do you have in place?

- Have you worked with single parents or unmarried couples successfully in the past? What percent of your adoptions are by singles or unmarried couples?

- How are your fees structured? Can you provide a breakdown? When are the amounts due? What fees are not included in this?

- What is the average length of time for one of your adoptions, from initial application to finalization?

- How many placements do you make per year? How many did you make in the last year?

- Do you have infants available? What is the average age of children placed through your agency?

- What part of your fees is refundable if the adoption does not succeed?

- Please explain your home study process. How long does it take?

- Can you provide a list of approved social workers to use for the home study?

- Will you assist with a private adoption? What fees would apply?

- How are your birth mothers located and screened?

- Who makes the placement decision—the agency or the birth mother? How is placement decided?

- What is your position on open adoption? What kind of relationship do you encourage or suggest that birth parents and adoptive parents should have or strive for?

- Do you provide counseling for birth and adoptive parents? Is it mandatory? Are there additional fees for this? What is involved in the counseling process?

- What medical history information is provided to adoptive parents about the birth parents? Are birth mothers screened for HIV and other congenitally transferred conditions?

- If a potential adoptive parent turns down a birth mother, may they continue in the program and receive the next available placement?

- If the adoption for this particular child is not completed, can the expenses paid be transferred or rolled over to the adoption of another child?

- Do you have a grievance policy? If so, how does it work? If not, how are problems resolved?

In addition to asking questions of the agency, do some legwork. Call your state agency that licenses and monitors adoption agencies (your social services or family and children department) and ask for information about the agency, including its history and any complaints that have been filed against it. Ask to speak to an adoption specialist in the department and ask about the agency's reputation.

The average length of time for a domestic private adoption should be under two years. If an agency tells you a longer average wait, you should question it and consider other agencies.

When you are ready to sign up with an agency, make sure you get everything in writing so that there can be no confusion or dispute. You will need to sign a contract with the agency, and it will spell out fees, procedures, and responsibilities. Make sure you have your adoption attorney review the contract before you sign it.

How to Afford Adoption

When considering adoption, many people are surprised by the costs involved. It may seem as if giving a child a home should not be such an expensive proposition. However, adoption is not always as expensive as it might seem. Foster care adoptions (state-agency adoptions) in particular are very affordable, since the state may handle most or all of the fees.

There are also ways to make private-agency adoption more affordable. You can purchase adoption insurance, which will reimburse you for out-of-pocket expenses if a planned adoption does not take place (if you do not have this and your agency does not have a policy of rolling over fees should this happen, you cannot recoup your costs). You can also apply for special low-interest loans available for prospective adoptive parents. For more information about adoption insurance and loans, contact:

- National Adoption Foundation: *www.nafadopt.org*

- The National Endowment for Financial Education offers helpful information about affording adoption: *www.nefe.org/adoption/*

Once you have adopted a child, you're entitled to up to a $10,000 federal tax deduction for the expenses of your adoption that you have not been reimbursed for. If you adopt a child with special needs, you are entitled to the full deduction (with some income restrictions) without having to show expenses. Additionally, if you can't take the full deduction in the year of your adoption, you can carry forward (take in later years) the remaining amounts. Talk to your accountant or tax preparer about this credit. Second-parent adoptions (where your partner adopts a child you are already the legal parent of) do not qualify.

Once your child has been adopted, you can list him or her as a dependant on your taxes, so make sure you let your tax preparer know about the adoption. Some states also offer adoption tax credits, so inquire about this.

Many employers offer adoption expense reimbursement (a 2004 survey found that 39 percent of the top 936 U.S. employers provided some kind of assistance). Check with your human resource manager to find out if your company offers such a program. Some employers offer a lump-sum payment of an amount between $1,000 and $15,000. Other employers pay for specific adoption expenses, such as agency or legal fees. You can view a list of employers who offer adoption benefits at *www.adoptionfriendlyworkplace.org.*

The Home Study

Once you've selected an agency (if you will be working with an agency) and signed on with them, the next important step is a home study. A home study is an evaluation and investigation by a licensed social worker of a prospective parent's background, parenting ability, home, and lifestyle.

It's important to be honest when talking with the social worker and filling out forms for her or him. If you have a partner and live together, share this information. Your partner is an important person in your life. Lying for the home study could place your entire adoption in jeopardy, so it is best to be as truthful as possible.

Home studies are required in almost all adoptions, but in some states they are waived for second-parent adoptions. If you adopt a child and then your partner chooses to go through a second-parent adoption where you need a home study, be sure to use the same social worker for both, since it will make the process much simpler.

If you are working with an agency, it can most likely provide a list of social workers it works with, or the agency may have in-house social workers who will perform the study. You can also find a social worker on your own; just make sure the social worker you use is licensed in your state. To read a sample adoption home study online, go to *www.1-800-homestudy.com/homestudy/sample.*

As part of the home study process, the social worker will come to your home, meet you and your partner (if you have one), and ask you questions about your background. He or she will ask about your family, where you have lived, where you were born, your education and job history, previous marriages, other children you have, and arrests or convictions.

To get a picture of your support system, the social worker will also ask questions about your lifestyle and personal life, including your work schedule, health, income, friends, and family. The social worker will inquire about organizations you belong to, pets, religion, hobbies and interests, smoking, drinking, and drug use. You'll be asked why you want to adopt, how you will fit a child into your life and home, what kind of childcare plans you will make, and how you will afford a child.

The social worker will want to see where you live and where the child will sleep. You don't need to have a nursery or bedroom decorated and ready for a child. All you need to do is show you have a room or space that will work. Your home doesn't have to be spotless, and it doesn't have to look like your typical middle-class family home. It just needs to be clear that a child would fit in there.

You may need to meet with the social worker more than once to cover all the information that is needed. Don't become overwhelmed by this process. Some prospective parents spend weeks repainting the house and decorating a nursery. This is not necessary. Your home should simply be relatively clean and neat. This isn't a contest to decide who would be the best parent. The home study is simply a way of making sure you're decent people who are able to care for a child. You're not going to flunk this test.

You will be asked to write an autobiographical statement, which basically restates the information you gave to the social worker during your in-person meetings. You will need to provide certified copies of birth and marriage certificates (if you were ever married, as well as divorce decrees) and a medical report from your physician describing your health and explaining any conditions you have. You also need written proof of your income (pay stubs and/or tax returns).

You will need to provide references as part of the home study process. Three to five people who know you well need to write letters and say positive things about you. Use a variety of people such as friends, neighbors, clergy, coworkers, and so on. They will be asked to explain how they know you, how long they have known you, and why they believe you would make a good adoptive parent.

You will need to be fingerprinted and/or have a criminal background check done. If your state requires fingerprints, you will be given a card or paperwork and told to go to your local police station to be fingerprinted. A background check requires you to complete a form with your name, address, and social security number. This is run through a computer to check for convictions, child abuse problems, or outstanding warrants.

There is generally a separate fee for the home study (which can range from $700 to $2,000 or a bit above). If you work with an agency, this fee may not be included in the fees you pay the agency. Once the investigation has been completed, the social worker will write a report that describes you and includes a recommendation as to whether you should adopt. The entire home study process can take anywhere from a few weeks to a few months, depending how quickly things can be scheduled and how soon you get the needed paperwork in.

Be sure to ask for a copy of the home study. It will be valid for one year to eighteen months. If you should switch agencies or change your plan, you'll need it. If your adoption isn't completed in that time frame, you might need to have it updated—a shorter and less expensive process.

Consent

Consent is the legal agreement by the birth parent(s) that the child can be adopted. If there are no living birth parents or the child was abandoned (as is often the case in international adoptions), then consent is given by the state or country the child is a resident of. Consent is absolutely essential in adoption, and it must include procedures to make sure birth parents are given adequate time to make the decision. If the consent to your adoption is not completely legal, problems can arise after the fact. This is why you sometimes hear stories of birth parents changing their minds or adoptions having to be reversed. If you're working with an agency, this usually isn't a problem. But if you're doing a private (nonagency) adoption, it's extremely important that you have an attorney who is experienced in handling this type of adoption and who can make sure the consent to your adoption is bulletproof.

👫 Life **Lessons**

Vicki and Ben were partners who shared a home. After trying to get pregnant for many years, they finally decided they wanted to adopt. At first, they were worried that they would not be able to adopt a child because they were not married and did not intend to get married. But Vicki went to an informational meeting at an adoption agency and learned that not being married would probably not interfere with their desire to become a family. They decided they wanted to do a private domestic agency adoption because they wanted to raise their child from birth. They decided that Vicki would be the one to adopt the child and that Ben would later do a second-parent adoption. They were most nervous about the home study, but the social worker was friendly and assured them that it didn't matter that they lived together. Once their application and home study were completed, they waited and waited for a baby. They got a call that there was a birth mother available but that she wanted to meet them. It was a very difficult meeting for Vicki and Ben, as they sat there thinking that that could be their baby inside the birth mother's stomach. Ultimately, the birth mother decided she was not comfortable with an unmarried couple. She felt strongly that her baby should be placed with a mom and a dad who were married. Vicki and Ben were upset, but tried to stay positive. Soon they met another birth mother, and she liked them. It seemed like forever until their baby was born, but finally their son arrived. Vicki was allowed to visit him at the hospital. In the days after the birth, the birth mother seemed to be wavering about the adoption, and there were a few tense moments, but eventually she did sign the consent and the adoption was finalized. Vicki and Ben brought their son home. The next year, Ben went through a second-parent adoption procedure and now they are the proud and happy and very legal parents of their beautiful son.

The birth mother, if she is alive or known, must consent to the adoption. The birth father must also provide consent, but only if paternity has been established. Paternity can be established through a formal legal admission by the father or through a court proceeding in which paternity is proven. Many states also have what is called a putative father registry. This is a place where a man can register if he believes he is the father of a child. Before a child is placed for adoption, the putative father registry must be searched. If someone has registered, paternity will be tested.

In most states, older children that are adopted must give their own consent to the adoption (this normally comes into play when a child is adopted out of foster care). The age at which a child must consent is usually ten, twelve, or fourteen, depending on the state.

Notice

Before a birth parent can give consent, he or she has to have notice of the adoption. Notice is accomplished by a legal procedure. Often a birth father may not be part of the child's life or may not be able to be located to give consent. In these cases, the court will direct that legal notice is given to him. Legal notice is specified in your state's laws and can include sending certified letters or court documents to his last known address or workplace or publishing a notice in a newspaper selected by the court. If the father does not respond, he is presumed to have waived his right to oppose the adoption. If notice is required in your adoption, your attorney will take careful steps to make sure it is done correctly. If notice is not given properly, the birth father could later come back and seek custody, so it is essential that this be done carefully and correctly.

There are specific time frames in which a birth mother must consent in order for the adoption to be legal. Formal, legal consent is usually required after the birth of the child. If a state allows consent before the birth, there is usually a requirement that the birth mother reaffirm her consent after the birth, before the adoption is made legal. The waiting period between the birth and the date when the birth mother's consent becomes final can vary from twelve hours after the birth to fifteen days after the birth.

Birth parent consent can be done in writing (usually notarized) in some states. Other states require that it be done in court—either by appearing personally in court or by filing certain papers with the court.

Revocation is the legal withdrawal of consent by a birth parent who previously gave legal consent (note that this is different from a mother changing her mind and deciding after the birth that she doesn't want to place the baby for adoption—that happens before consent has been finalized). You've probably heard horror stories about adoptions being revoked at the last minute. Revocation is actually difficult to do. A few states do not allow any revocation under any circumstances. Other states permit revocation only if there has been fraud, coercion, or other factors that show the birth parent did not have complete knowledge of the adoption or have free will at the time of the consent. A few states allow birth parents to change their minds for any reason within a certain time period, but this can only happen within that time period. When that stated time period has elapsed, there's no possibility of the court overturning the adoption because a birth mother changed her mind and now wants her baby back. Once the court has completely finalized the adoption, the adoption cannot be revoked.

Adoption Court Procedure

The actual court procedure for an adoption is your final step. When you get to this point, there should be some relief because you've gotten through the waiting and you have also met your child. Revocation of consent is the only real worry facing prospective adoptive parents at this point, and this is an unlikely scenario.

Adoptions are finalized by your state's family, juvenile, or surrogate's court. Your attorney will file your adoption petition and other paperwork and a date will be scheduled for the adoption. The court will review all the documents, including the home study and background checks. If the birth parent(s) is required to or chooses to give consent in front of the judge, this will happen in the courtroom. If the child is of the age set by the state, he or she will be asked to consent to the adoption. If a birth father could not be located and notice was given, the court will review the notice to make sure it meets the state's requirements. The adoption is then finalized and the judge signs the final order, making it official and legal. The actual court appearance is really just a formality. There is no trial and no questioning or cross-examination. If a problem with your adoption should happen, your attorney would be notified before the court date and the problem would be solved in advance.

Judges spend most of their time dealing with cases where people are arguing or are unhappy, so it is a pleasant experience for them to handle an adoption where the result is a happy ending. Most judges will allow family and friends to join you in the courtroom, making it possible for you to bring your partner, even if he or she is not adopting with you at this time. Photos may be permitted. The court staff will often congratulate the adoptive parents and ooh and ahh over the adoptive child. If the adoptive child is old enough to speak and understand what is happening, he or she is often made a part of the proceeding as well and is made to feel as if something very special has happened for him or her. Some judges will even give the child a certificate or a card to commemorate the special day. If you don't want to bring your child, you may not have to; you can ask if the child's presence is required. However, most parents feel the child should be there for such an important occasion.

Post Placement

With most agency adoptions, you will have some post-placement contact with the agency or with a social worker. There may be one or two of these post-placement visits from the social worker to make sure things are going smoothly and to offer assistance with adjustments. These visits are nothing to worry about and are just procedure. The worker will prepare a post-placement report, which is filed with the agency and may be filed with the court if required in your state.

Birth Certificates

After the adoption is finalized, you will receive an amended birth certificate for your adopted child that lists the new parents (or parent if you are adopting alone), but maintains the child's birth date. This will be your child's official, legal birth certificate, and it will have no indication on it that an adoption took place—it looks like a regular birth certificate. The old birth certificate still exists as a state record, but it is not accessible. The adoption court proceeding also becomes sealed and not accessible. This is why you hear about adult adoptees having difficulty finding their birth parents. The information about the birth becomes inaccessible to protect privacy.

What to Expect When Adopting as an Unmarried Couple

Except in the states specifically mentioned in Chapter 4, you will need to adopt as a two-part process, since few states allow an unmarried couple to adopt simultaneously. When you go about adopting a child this way, you can expect to be asked questions about your living situation and who you live with. If you live with your partner, it is important to be honest about this. There may be some questions about why you are not married or planning to marry. Answer those questions honestly.

Advocacy Tip

Write to your state government representatives if you believe that unmarried couples should be able to adopt simultaneously. Explain your own personal situation and show how this law has made your life difficult and is not fair to your child. Putting a face on this issue can make it real for your representative.

Birth mothers may want to know your specific plans and whether your partner will adopt your child once the first adoption is complete. If so, it is likely the birth mothers will want to meet and get to know your partner, even though he or she is not part of the actual first adoption in a legal way. There are some birth mothers who may be uncomfortable with your unmarried status as a couple, and this could make finding a child more difficult to do through a private agency that has an open adoption policy.

What to Expect When Adopting Alone

When you adopt as a single person, you welcome a child into your home and plan to be his or her sole parent. Adoption agencies and birth mothers may see you as being at a disadvantage, so you may need to offer reassurances about your plans.

The primary concern of birth mothers and agencies is that you have backup. This means that you have friends and family who will support you and help you raise your child. You can also offer information about daycare centers, nannies, or sitters you will make arrangements with. There may be some concern about your ability to financially support a child, so showing financial stability is important, and making plans that include life and disability insurance can be an added bonus.

Talking to Your Child about Adoption

There are a variety of very good books for children about adoption that you can read to your child as a way of introducing and beginning a conversation about adoption (see Appendix B for specific recommendations). Many parents find that it is helpful to talk about the adoption with the child from the very beginning so that it is never big news you have to suddenly deliver. Share age-appropriate information with your child and answer his or her questions as best you can. Some parents celebrate their child's adoption day as well as the child's birthday as a special way of commemorating the way the child came into the family.

If you are part of a couple and only one of you is the child's legal parent, at some point you'll need to explain this and why it is so. If both of you are the child's emotional parents, however, it is important to make it clear to the child that you are both parents in the same way, in every aspect except the legal one.

Many children want to meet their biological parents. Experts agree that unless the biological parent has been incorporated into the family structure from the beginning, finding the biological parent is not recommended until the child becomes an adult. Once the child is an adult, he or she can seek out and meet the biological parent if that birth parent wants to have contact.

Chapter 7
Assisted Conception and Unmarried Parents

If you want to start a family but have been unable to conceive on your own, assisted conception is an avenue available to you, or you and your partner. Assisted conception includes fertility treatments as well as options such as sperm and egg donations, embryo donation, and surrogacy.

Your Right to Medical Assistance

Most clinics and physicians will not deny you treatment because you are single, but unmarried status is not a protected category in terms of illegal discrimination, so there may be some physicians who may choose not to treat you because they are morally opposed to assisting single people to conceive. You cannot legally compel them to treat you.

It is likely that you will be asked if you are married when you complete paperwork to enter the practice as a new patient. This is often done for billing purposes and also for emergency notification purposes. It is your choice whether to answer this question. It is unlikely anyone will notice if you leave it blank. If you have a partner, you have the option of listing him or her as "spouse" on this paperwork. Most reproductive endocrinologists are used to treating married couples and will simply assume you are married unless told otherwise. If you wish to make that distinction, it is up to you.

Advocacy Tip

Should you encounter a doctor or clinic that refuses to treat you because of your marital status, there are things you can do. Notify the administration if you are seeking treatment at a clinic, hospital, or practice and one physician denies you treatment. Write a letter detailing the date, situation, and circumstances. You can also directly confront the person denying you treatment and ask specifically why you are being denied. Make it a point to tell the physician that you will be sure to spread the word about this facility's unfriendliness.

Should you encounter a medical professional who does not wish to help you with conception, there are plenty of other physicians out there who will, so find someone else. In most cases, you probably don't want to work with someone who is hostile to unmarried people anyhow.

Types of Assisted Conception

There are a variety of ways to use medical assistance to create a family. All of them bring you to the same result—a child in your arms. It's important to choose the path that is right for your family. Before making a decision, gather information about the options available to you and consider what path you are most comfortable with.

Fertility Treatments

There are a wide variety of fertility treatments available. If you go in for a fertility workup, generally the approach is to treat the couple together. Both partners are initially tested to try to isolate where a problem might lie. Fertility testing can be stressful for both partners, both because often each partner is worried about being "at fault," and also because it is stressful to discuss your personal life and have your reproductive functioning measured. When you enter into fertility treatment, you give up some of your privacy, and this can be difficult or uncomfortable for some people.

The fact that you and your partner are not married should have no impact on the type of testing you receive or the type of treatment that is recommended for you. Some types of treatment require close reliance on a partner, such as women who need daily hormone shots performed by a partner or some other assistance on a daily basis.

Because fertility testing and treatment can take months or years, it is important to find a way to balance the stress you feel through the course of the medical treatment. It is also important not to lose sight of your personal or sexual relationship, even though you may feel as though it is under a microscope or tightly scheduled. Fertility treatments are a means to an end, and it's essential to keep your perspective, continue to be spontaneous when possible, make time for your relationship, and not allow the treatments to take over your entire life.

Insemination

There are two types of insemination that are possible in fertility treatments. Many couples undergoing fertility treatments progress beyond hormone pills or shots and move on to intrauterine insemination. In this process, the man's sperm is inserted directly into the woman's uterus, to increase the chances of conceiving. Because you are not married, the clinic or physician may ask that the man sign a consent form, permitting the use of his sperm for this procedure. There may be some confusion about your intent because often when a man and woman are not married, the man is acting as a sperm donor and is asked to sign an agreement giving up all his rights to the child. You certainly do not want to do that, so make sure that you carefully read any consent forms.

Donor insemination is another option, and is a common choice for single women and lesbian couples, as well as heterosexual couples who have encountered a male fertility problem. When you use donor sperm, you can choose a donor through a sperm bank or you can use a known donor, such as a relative or close friend. You can read a booklet about insemination from the American Society of Reproductive Medicine at *www.asrm.org/Literature/patient.html.*

The advantage of a known donor is that you not only know the person (as well as his medical history, personality, and traits) and have some kind of relationship, but also you can create a relationship of your choosing for your child to share with the donor. There are a variety of roles the donor can play in your child's life, and those involved can create whatever arrangement feels right, although these arrangements are usually informal and are not legal. Another advantage of a known donor is that should the donor or one of his close family members be later diagnosed with a genetic disease, you will know about it and can use that information to protect your child's health.

Using a known donor has disadvantages as well. Should you choose to involve the donor openly in your child's life, it is possible that he or you could at some point become dissatisfied with the relationship— for example, expecting more or less than the other person or people involved. If you are friends, the donation could in some way affect your friendship in the future. More and more singles and couples are creating nontraditional families that include biological parents as part of the structure, but it is still unfamiliar territory to many people. It can be difficult to create a family structure like this if you've never encountered a similar one. The best advice is to be honest with everyone involved, develop a level of trust, and clearly spell out what everyone's roles will be.

When using a known donor, it is essential that he be tested for sexually transmitted diseases, especially HIV, even if everyone is certain he will get a clean bill of health. It is usually recommended that everyone involved in the insemination (donor, woman, and her partner, if any) obtain counseling prior to the procedure to help work through any potential problems. It is essential that you discuss the donor's role in the child's life in advance and come to an understanding about it.

Even if you and the donor have a relationship of some kind (friends or family), it is important to have a reproductive rights attorney draw up a legally binding insemination agreement. This agreement will protect everyone involved. In the agreement, the donor will formally give up all legal rights to the child, including custody or visitation. This is essential so that he can never change his mind and decide he wants to be a real parent to the child. The donor is released from any financial obligations to the child, such as child support. If the woman has a partner, it is a good idea to have him or her also sign the agreement, since the intention is that he (or she) will become a legal parent of the child. The woman's partner will need to adopt the child to become a legal parent.

An unknown donor is located through a sperm bank. Sperm banks pay donors for sperm and carefully screen all donors for sexually transmitted diseases. Complete medical histories are available, and a woman or couple can select a donor based on physical characteristics, occupation, IQ, and many other identifying traits. Donor sperm is frozen and preserved carefully until it is dispensed for use. The woman or couple using the sperm must pay a fee for the sperm specimens.

Because there is no U.S. federal regulation of sperm banks, make sure you use one licensed by your state or accredited by the American Association of Tissue Banks (*www.aatb.org*). Sperm banks should monitor the numbers of offspring of each donor in order to keep those numbers in check (too many offspring from one donor increases the risk of siblings meeting and having children together without realizing they share the same father). Always ask if the bank monitors this—a good bank will. It may be possible to buy all the donations from one donor to ensure that no one has a child related to yours, but it could get expensive, depending on how many deposits were made and if the donor is still an active donor. If you are interested in having other children, ask about reserving additional sperm from the same donor for future use so that your children can be biological siblings.

Sperm banks have written agreements with the donors that remove all of the donors' rights. The woman will also sign a contract with the sperm bank, which should be reviewed by an attorney.

When a woman uses insemination to become pregnant, she is the legal mother of the child when he or she is born. Even if the woman's partner provided the sperm, legal paternity procedures must be followed to make him the father. If donor sperm is used, the woman's partner can adopt the child after the birth.

Egg Donation

Egg donation is a process available for women who don't ovulate or who cannot get pregnant with their own eggs. A donor woman provides eggs, and her eggs are inseminated in an IVF (in vitro fertilization) procedure and then implanted in the intended mother. The woman who gives birth to the child is not genetically related to the baby, but is the legal mother. Some women choose this procedure because it allows them to carry the pregnancy and bond in that way with the child.

Some women are able to ask friends or family members to donate eggs, while others use anonymous donors who are financially compensated for their donation. Some clinics have egg donor programs, where couples undergoing IVF donate their extra eggs, often in return for a fee reduction. When using anonymous donors through the clinic, there is often little selection available, when you compare to the numbers of sperm donors available. Egg donors must undergo hormone treatment and a surgical extraction, so there are far fewer people willing to undergo this procedure. It is also possible to locate a donor on your own, such as through newspaper ads.

Another complication with egg donation compared to sperm donation is that eggs do not freeze well. Therefore, the donor woman and the intended mother have to synchronize their cycles so that the intended mother's body is ready to have an embryo implanted at the same time that the donor's body is ready to do so.

Both donor and recipient (and her partner, if any) need to undergo medical testing as well as counseling. The cost of egg donation is slightly more than the cost of IVF. It is essential that both parties sign an agreement with the clinic, clearly laying out legal parentage and waivers of rights. Under the agreement, the donor has no right to ever claim custody or visitation and is freed from any obligation to pay child support. The recipient's partner should also sign the agreement.

If the intended mother's partner provides the sperm for the procedure, he will need to have his parentage recognized through an acknowledgment of paternity. If he does not provide sperm, he will need to adopt the child after the birth.

Embryo Donation

Embryo donation occurs when a fertilized egg from another couple is donated to a woman or couple who will carry the pregnancy and become legal parents of the child. These embryos are extras that were created when another couple went through IVF. They can be frozen and preserved for future use if the couple wants more children. Some couples decide their families are complete and release these embryos for donation to other couples. This is not a common procedure—a recent survey located only fifty-three children born through this process in the United States.

Embryo donation allows a woman or couple to have a family and experience pregnancy without going through adoption. The donors and recipients sign agreements with the clinic waiving all rights and responsibilities of the intended parents. The woman who gives birth to the child is the legal parent from the moment of birth. Her partner can adopt the child.

Embryo donation is also sometimes called embryo adoption, and an adoption agency is involved in the process. The donor parents get to select the intended parents, and a home study is done.

Surrogacy

Surrogacy is a process in which a surrogate carries the pregnancy and the intended parents become the child's parents. There are two types of surrogacy. In traditional surrogacy, the surrogate's own eggs are used and the pregnancy is usually achieved through insemination. In gestational surrogacy, the intended mother's eggs are harvested and inseminated with the father's sperm and then implanted into the surrogate using IVF.

In both processes, the intended father becomes the legal father after a paternity proceeding, and the intended mother must adopt the child to become a legal parent. A few states, such as California, have a legal process set up to handle surrogacy, and paperwork for parentage can be completed prior to the birth of the child.

When using surrogacy, it is crucial that you retain an attorney experienced in this area. Many surrogates are located through specialized surrogacy agencies, although it is possible to use a known surrogate (friend or family member) or find a surrogate on your own. Counseling is an important part of the surrogacy process, and generally the surrogate and intended parents develop some kind of relationship through the pregnancy, which they may agree to continue in some way after the child is born.

The legal agreement that is signed by all the parties (including the surrogate's own husband, if any, since he would be the child's legal father at birth if the agreement were not in place) is of utmost importance. Your attorney can advise you as to the laws of the state in which you are entering into the agreement and what the allowable expenses and costs are that you can pay for (many states do not allow payment for surrogacy or restrict the types and amounts of expenses the intended parents can pay for). It is crucial that your agreement be carefully written and within your state's laws.

Many people, when they think of surrogacy, remember famous cases, such as Baby M, in which the surrogate changes her mind and wants to keep the baby herself. These cases are more likely in traditional surrogacy, where the surrogate is genetically related to the child. Even if the surrogate should have a change of heart, however, the intended father is still the baby's legal and biological father and will have an excellent case for custody. No one wants to face this kind of heartache, though, which is why it is important to choose your surrogate carefully and go through a counseling process that will allow everyone involved to be certain about the process.

Unused Embryos

If your fertility treatment includes IVF, a process in which eggs are harvested from the mother and inseminated with sperm from the father, it is likely you may have additional embryos left over after each treatment. These embryos can be frozen for future use—for later cycles during your current attempt at pregnancy or for use years later if you want to have more than one child.

It is a good idea to talk with your partner about these frozen embryos and what your intentions toward them are. Some clinics ask parents to sign a document authorizing the release of unneeded embryos for scientific testing, for donation to other infertile couples, or to be destroyed after a certain period of time. There have been a few cases in which married couples have fought over "custody" of frozen embryos in a divorce, as well as what their rights and responsibilities are to any children that result from later impregnation with these embryos. It is conceivable that an unmarried couple could experience the same kind of conflict should they separate and not be able to agree about ownership, use, or disposal of the embryos. You and your partner can include your wishes in the agreement with the clinic, or you could write and sign an agreement together and have it notarized (or prepared by your attorney), stating what your intent for the unused embryos is. Because you both supplied the genetic material for the embryos, you both have legal ownership rights to the embryos, and the fact that you are not married has no impact on that. Reaching an agreement now about unused embryos could save a lot of time, money, and heartache later.

Talking to Your Child about Assisted Conception

In general, assisted conception is not something your child is going to know about unless you introduce the topic. If you used fertility treatments to get pregnant, it's probably not something you'll want or need to discuss with your child until he or she is much older. If you used donor material to create your family, you may decide this is information you want your child to have at some point. It will be important for your child to understand the medical history implications when he or she is an adult. This is a topic you can introduce gradually as you answer your child's questions with age-appropriate answers. When your five-year-old asks you where babies come from, it's too much information to talk about the details of insemination or IVF; however, it may be appropriate to talk about mommies and daddies loving each other and babies growing from special eggs or seeds in the mommy's tummy. It is also appropriate to talk about other people helping those babies to grow, or babies growing in other women's tummies. Tailor your responses to your child's ability to understand. Details should gradually emerge as your child ages.

👫 Life **Lessons**

Kate and Michael had lived together for five years and had been trying to start a family for two years. Because Kate was over thirty-five, her gynecologist suggested she see a reproductive endocrinologist. She scheduled an appointment and was told that both of them needed to go. The office did not ask if they were married at any point. The endocrinologist met with them and asked a lot of questions about their medical histories, reproductive histories, and sex life. They began with a battery of tests and learned that IVF was the best option for them. It took them several months to save the $10,000 they needed for the IVF cycle. The cycle was not successful. They were crushed. They met with the doctor again and then took a few weeks to consider their options. They borrowed money from family and tried another cycle, again with no success. Kate was exhausted, both physically and emotionally. Michael felt the emotional strain as well. They found the money for one more cycle, and again had no success.

The doctor did not recommend another cycle and felt their chances of success were slim. Kate was deeply depressed at this point. Michael was ready to move on and consider adoption, but Kate had not reached that point. They spent several months thinking and healing. Then, they talked to a surrogacy agency. They agreed they would try one cycle with a surrogate before turning to adoption. The agency introduced them to a married surrogate who had two children of her own and had been a surrogate for two other couples. She was ready to help them. Kate and Michael felt comfortable with her.

Kate and Michael hired an attorney who helped work out the surrogacy agreement. The agreement specified that the surrogate and her husband would not be the legal parents of the child and that Kate and Michael would instead be the legal parents. It also listed the expenses Kate and Michael would pay during her pregnancy. Kate and Michael agreed to do gestational surrogacy with her. Kate underwent yet another hormone induced cycle and had her eggs harvested and fertilized with Michael's sperm. The embryos were implanted in the surrogate and, happily, a pregnancy resulted.

Because Kate and Michael lived in California and the surrogacy contract took place there, their attorney was able to begin a surrogacy proceeding in California court before the baby was born. Because Kate's eggs were used, the surrogate could legally relinquish her rights before the birth. A court order was in place naming Kate and Michael as legal parents (permissible in California, even though they were not married). The baby was born and the birth certificate was issued in Kate and Michael's names. The surrogate was pleased to have been able to help them become parents. They sent her photos a few times a year and kept in touch by e-mail. They planned to someday tell their child how the surrogate had helped them and hoped she would have a role as a special aunt in their child's life.

Chapter 8

Parents and Partners: Parenting as an Unmarried Couple

Having a child together as a couple changes the dynamics of your relationship, as well as your economic situation and your day-to-day life. No matter how your child enters you life—through birth or adoption—the child creates tremendous change in your lives.

Now there is another person whose needs take precedence over yours and your partner's. This change can place a strain on even the most solid of relationships, but it can also allow your relationship to bloom in ways you never imagined. As your child grows, you'll find that your relationship must adjust to accommodate the changes in your child's life.

Parenting in the Same Household

If you and your partner share a residence, you'll make many decisions together about your child. Whether you're parenting a newborn or an older child, deciding how you share your time with your child—if one parent will spend more time at home, if you'll need to hire a sitter or daycare, or if you will flex your schedules—is an important consideration. You'll also need to make adjustments in other aspects of your lives, such as living space and finances.

Advocacy Tip

Many people still tend to make the distinction between children born in a marriage and those born "out of wedlock." This is really an antiquated concept and one that can be changed if people can come to understand that when a child is born, it creates a family, and that is the concept we should all focus on.

Organizing Your Household

When a child comes into your lives, you need to make physical accommodations for him or her. Transitioning a couple's space into a family home can be a difficult change. If you are adding an infant to your family, the changes will happen gradually, but if you're adding an older child through adoption or foster care, getting used to the space your child takes up is a change. If you and a partner are just beginning to live together and one of you already has a child, there are many adjustments to be made for all of you. Plan ahead as much as you can, but plan to be flexible as everyone in the home adjusts to the new arrangements.

Housing

This is a good time to give some thought to your living arrangement overall. If you are renting, are you both on the lease or is it in only one name? If you own a home, is only one name on the deed? While it may be simpler to leave things as they are, you may wish to consider joint tenancy or ownership of your home. You might find that now is the time to move to a bigger space or to purchase a home. However, moving is stressful in and of itself, and moving when your family is growing is even more stressful.

Many couples find that once they add a child to their relationship, they feel a need to become equal partners in their home as well. Remember, though, that once you place both names on a lease, you are both legally responsible for paying the rent, and once you place both names on a deed, you become equal owners in the property. Placing a name on the deed does not change the legal responsibility for the mortgage. If you want both names on the mortgage, you need to refinance. Once you add a name to the mortgage, there is no easy way to take it off and you have to refinance again to change that.

Responsibilities

Another important part of organizing your household is thinking about how you will divide responsibilities with regard to your child. One parent may find it easier to handle nighttime feedings than the other; one parent may be more comfortable taking the child to play groups and so on. It's important to look to your individual abilities, qualities, and needs and not to rely on what you think you should be doing, what other people make you feel you should be doing, or on gender stereotypes. If you are new to parenting, you'll find that you adjust as things come up and that you absolutely can't plan out everything.

🚹🚹 Life Lessons

Trina and Mark were expecting a baby. Neither one of them felt that they should rush into marriage because the baby was coming, so they decided to keep the status quo for now. If they were going to get married, Trina was certainly not going to do it in a maternity wedding gown. But now that the baby was coming, Trina felt funny living at Mark's apartment. After all, it was his space. He picked it out, he signed the lease, and he had all of his furniture there. When Trina moved in with him, it had been so they could be together, but neither one of them thought about it as a long-term solution. They discussed it and decided to move to an apartment with an extra bedroom for the baby. They also planned to start saving to buy a house. They would bring Mark's furniture but also use some furniture Trina had inherited from her grandmother. Trina felt so relieved to be moving to a place that would be "theirs" instead of "his" and would have room for the baby. Everything seemed much more settled and real to her.

Dealing with Expenses

You also should examine how you are dividing income and expenses. A child brings additional expenses, and you'll need to make arrangements as to how you will divide these between you. You might choose to share all expenses evenly, each take on full responsibility for specific expenses, or have one parent carry most of the household costs, depending on your incomes and what feels right to the two of you. The problem with dividing or sharing child-related expenses is that it can be hard to pinpoint what exactly is a child-related expense and what is a household expense. Groceries, for example, are both a child-related and a household expense, and it could be argued that rent is as well. It is best to have a complete plan for how you will share or divide all household expenses so that you don't have to have arguments about what falls into which category.

You can also get a court order of child support at this point if you would feel more comfortable (see Chapter 2). You don't need to live in separate homes for child support laws to apply. However, before you can get a determination of child support, you will need an order deciding custody/parenting time. You can simply stipulate joint custody.

This is also a good time to make a budget. You need to calculate exactly how much money each of you brings into the home and then you need to add up all of your expenses. You might find it helpful to take a week or a month and write down everything that you spend money on. This will give you an accurate picture of how much you're spending. Once you do this, you can create an accurate budget and take a look at where you can cut back, how you can save money, and what might be the best way to divide expenses.

Another important decision has to do with taxes—which parent will claim the child as a dependent. As an unmarried couple, you must file separately. Only one parent may claim the child as a deduction. It usually makes sense to evaluate which one of you can benefit from this the most. Talk to an accountant or tax preparer if you need help determining this.

Possible Strategies for Sharing Parenting Expenses

- Create a joint account to which you both contribute to pay child-related expenses.

- Divide child-related expenses so that you each pay some of these fully.

- Split all child-related expenses evenly.

- Prorate expense sharing based on your respective incomes.

- Agree that one parent will handle all expenses.

Talking to Your Child about Your Relationship

When children reach age four or five (and often even at younger ages), they ask questions and compare their lives and families to those they observe. At some point, your child will realize that you and the other parent aren't married and that many other parents are. Answer your child's questions and use them as a guide to what your child is concerned about. Try to anticipate what some of the questions will be and think through what your answers will be in advance so you aren't caught off guard. Children are most concerned with knowing that they and their family are secure and that they are loved. Those are the primary concerns your child will have.

Talk about what marriage is and talk about what your relationship is and how the two differ and are the same. If you are gay, explain that the laws of your state don't allow gay partners to legally marry each other or explain that you have a domestic partnership agreement. If you are a heterosexual couple, explain why you choose not to marry and point out how your relationship is committed without it. If you are not a couple but do live together, explain that both of you love him or her very much and are parents together even if you are not a married or intimate couple.

Give an explanation that is appropriate to your child's age. A four-year-old won't understand the difference between a domestic partnership and marriage, but is able to understand love and commitment. One way to explain it would be to say "we don't need anyone to tell us we're your parents and that we love you, and we don't need anyone to tell the two of us that we love each other and belong together." If you're honest with your child and give an explanation that you are comfortable with, you'll find that your child will accept your explanation. Encourage him or her to ask questions, as this allows you to direct the conversation to his or her concerns.

You might say:

- The three of us are a family, and that means we take care of each other and belong together.

- Mom and I love each other and live with each other, but we aren't married. We don't think we need to be married to love each other. Other people do and that's okay for them.

- Sometimes when two people love each other, they decide to stay together forever. Dad and I decided that. In our state you can only get married if you are a boy and girl. Dad and I are boys so we aren't married, but we did promise to be together.

Avoid saying:

- Marriage is just a way of making women submit to men and of creating ownership of children.

- Marriage is a way of legalizing sex. No one should be able to tell us who we can have sex with.

- We aren't married because we think that it is our right to love each other without the government telling us we can.

- This country is completely homophobic and the thought of allowing gays to marry scares the heck out of straight people.

These kinds of statements are too much information and too complicated for children. Yes, you want to instill your political and social views in your child, but you have to do so in a slow and careful way.

Parenting in Separate Households

If you and your partner live in separate households but are still romantically involved, you'll need to make some adjustments in the way you relate to each other, spend time with each other, and organize your lives once you become parents. If you live separately and are not an intimate couple, see Chapter 9.

Dealing with Legalities

If you and your partner don't live in the same home, there can be confusion with regard to custody of your child. When this is the case, it is a good idea to get a formal order of custody from your local family court. This doesn't have to mean that one of you is taking the other to court, and it doesn't have to mean that one of you is trying to cut the other out of the child's life. You can agree to an order of joint custody and you needn't specify how you will each spend time with your child. You can even have an attorney draw up a stipulation so that you can resolve the entire matter with one court appearance. Having a court order is unfortunately necessary because once your child reaches school age, you'll have to specify custody for the school. It's also a good idea in case you and your partner should ever end your relationship.

Don't let yourself get tied up in or upset by the legal words and phrases. If you and your partner intend to parent together, go ahead and do it. Don't worry about what judges or lawyers think. This is your child and your family, and it is your absolute right to manage it and arrange it any way you choose.

Organizing Your Households

If you and your partner will continue to live in separate homes after becoming parents, there are a lot of adjustments to make to your homes. If your child will spend time at both homes, you'll need space for your child and some basic necessities at each place. It's not necessary to completely outfit two homes with children's supplies, nor is it necessary to transport everything back and forth.

The home where your child will spend most of his or her time should have a crib or a bed (depending on the child's age) and the other home can make do with a folding crib, cot, or even a sleeping bag, depending on your child's age. The more comfortable you can make it for your child, the better it will be. While a high chair for a baby or toddler is a good idea at the primary home, a booster seat or portable high chair could work well at the other home. It makes sense to have clothing, toys, and feeding supplies at both homes, so that you don't need to transport a lot with the child. If your child is going to be spending an equal amount of time at both homes, it may then be necessary to have two of each essential type of equipment.

If your child needs medication, some should be kept at each home. Additionally, the child's health insurance card or a copy should be in the possession of each parent.

Items to Transport with Your Child

Infants

- Pacifiers
- Special blanket
- Snowsuit or coat
- Favorite toys
- Extra diapers
- Breast milk if needed

Toddlers

- Special blanket and/or stuffed animals
- Coat
- Shoes
- Favorite toys
- Favorite DVDs or music

Elementary School Children

- School books
- Backpack
- Sneakers
- Sports uniforms/equipment
- Instruments
- School or scout uniforms
- Toys or hobbies

Preteens and Teens

- School books
- Personal organizer
- Laptop
- Uniforms and sports equipment
- Cell phone
- MP3 player
- Journal
- Preferred personal hygiene items

Continuing Your Relationship after You Have a Child

Although you and your partner primarily live in separate homes, you are romantically involved with each other and want to spend time together as a couple. You may find that it is difficult to schedule couple time once a child is in the picture. Consider getting a sitter, planning together time when your child is asleep, or scheduling time together as a family with your child. There will definitely be a period of adjustment, but just as parents do who live under the same roof, you'll find that you do manage to fall into a routine.

�$\mathbf{\Uparrow}$ Life Lessons

Mia and Robert have a four-year-old son named Chase and live in separate homes in the same city. Before their son was born, they spent most weekends together and had dinner together two or three times a week. Once Chase came along, it was really hard for them to adjust. When Chase was a baby, he needed a lot of attention. They would spend weekends as a family and have dinner a few times during the week but never felt as if they had any real time together alone. Sometimes Chase spent the night with Robert, but mostly he lived at Mia's house. Mia and Robert ended up doing most of their "couple time" on the phone at night after Chase was in bed. Soon they realized that they needed time alone together, as well as time as a family. Now Robert's mother spends every Wednesday afternoon and evening with Chase while Mia and Robert spend this time together. They continue to spend every weekend and one or two weekday evenings together as a family. Chase spends one night a week with Robert at his home. The arrangement works out perfectly for them.

Dealing with Expenses

You can choose to work out an expense-sharing arrangement on your own, or you can get assistance from a mediator or family court. Read Chapters 2 and 3 for explanations about child support laws. When you have a child together, even if you are unmarried and live separately, you're both responsible for supporting your child. You may feel that you don't need the involvement of a court and would feel more comfortable working out an arrangement on your own. This is your personal choice to make, and you should do whatever works best for your family. Remember that even if you choose not to obtain a child support order now, you can always do so in the future.

Sharing children's expenses when you live apart can be difficult. You may not be used to sharing expenses with each other if you are each maintaining your own home. When you live in separate homes, it can be particularly difficult to work out a fair way to share expenses. You both have completely separate expenses related to your own homes, and it may feel strange for one parent to give the other money if you have never been financially dependent on each other before. The best way to handle this is to sit down and discuss it together. Create your own separate budgets and then talk about the expenses a child is adding to each of your homes. You will probably find that one household is bearing more of the expense than the other. You can use this information to find a fair way for one parent to contribute money to the other parent's home to help manage these expenses.

You will also need to decide who will claim the child as a tax exemption. Only one of you may do so, so it makes sense to evaluate which one of you can benefit from this the most. Talk to your accountant or tax preparer if you need help calculating this. You can reassess this each year and change who takes the exemption each year if necessary.

There is no requirement that you share expenses or that one parent gives the other parent money. If this makes you uncomfortable or if you are both financially stable enough to be able to manage child-related expenses on your own, you can certainly do so. Sharing a family does not have to focus on sharing money. One of the reasons many divorced couples have such rancorous relationships is because a large part of their contact with each other is about exchanging money.

Talking to Your Child about Your Relationship

At some point your child will realize that his or her parents live in separate homes and that many other parents share a home. Most of the questions will be about the child's own situation. Kids want to know what will happen to them, to their room, their home, their schedule, and their life. Reassure your child by providing details about the practical aspects and exactly how things that affect him or her will be handled.

How you choose to explain your relationship is a matter of personal choice, but it's important to emphasize to your child that he or she has two loving parents. You'll need to explain the difference to your child between your relationship and relationships in which parents are divorced and live apart. Tailor your explanation to your child's age. A five-year-old won't understand explanations about personal freedom but will understand that you love each other and just like to live in separate houses. Young children are very nonjudgmental. When your child is older you may have a more difficult time gaining her unquestioning acceptance. In general though, if you can be honest and comfortable with the explanation you give your child, he or she will be satisfied with it.

Dealing with Parenting Conflicts

You and your partner will not always see eye to eye about how you want to raise your child or run your household(s). You may wish to set up some basic rules of play that will help guide your parenting relationship. Some parents find it helpful to write down these rules, while others find that just discussing them is enough. These rules or guidelines can include things such as agreeing not to make major decisions without discussing them with the other parent, agreeing to make medical decisions together, agreeing that whichever parent is present will handle emergency decisions, and so on.

Sample Basic Parenting/Household Rules

- We will consult each other before making major decisions about our child.

- We will try not to argue in front of our child.

- We agree to equally share the child's laundry responsibilities and will alternate weeks.

- We both believe it is reasonable for our child to sleep in the parent's bed at night when necessary.

- We do not believe in physical discipline.

- We will try not to judge or belittle the other person's parenting skills and decisions.

- We intend to raise our child as a vegetarian but are willing to make exceptions to this rule when necessary.

- We will try to allow each other some individual child-free time each week, but will be flexible about it.

- We will each try to cut back on our outings with friends so we can have more time together as a family.

- Susan would like to buy a house as a couple. Lee agrees that if we can save at least $10,000 for a down payment by next year, we will look for a house.

- Once a month we will balance our bank accounts and settle our accounts with each other.

- Chris will pay all grocery bills and Tim will pay all other household expenses as long as Chris is working part-time, which both agree is for the benefit of their child.

Working out Disputes

Even if you have some rules to follow to help you organize and plan out your relationship, you're going to have conflicts—every couple does. You may have conflicts about parenting or about things completely unrelated to parenting. The responsibility of parenting together can also strain other parts of your relationship that seem unrelated.

The best way to work out problems is to try to do so out of earshot of your child. All parents have disagreements, and it's okay for kids to know this (in fact, it's good for them to understand that two people who love each other can disagree, make up, and still love each other), but you don't want to work out all the details of your relationship in front of your child if you can avoid it. It is also best to try to keep conversations about money separate from your child. Children who overhear discussions or arguments about money can often feel guilty, believing that they are the source of the problem.

Getting angry can be unavoidable, but most of the time it won't help you solve your problems. It can be useful to tell your partner how you feel and let off steam, but most of the time you aren't going to be able to work out problems if you're yelling. If you can, try to talk about problems when both of you can be calm and have time to discuss the problem and possible solutions.

When you are an unmarried couple it can be easy to use your unmarried status as a weapon in an argument. Some unmarried parents who share a home with their partners threaten to move out and point out that there is nothing stopping them. If you and your partner are committed to each other, this is a weapon neither of you should use if you can help it. Doing so will not only cause deep hurt, but will also make your child feel very insecure.

Dealing with Instability

Some unmarried couples have a lot of instability in their relationship, and this can be one reason why they have chosen not to marry. Other couples remain happily unmarried in a very stable and committed relationship. If your relationship does have instability, it's important to understand that adding a child to the relationship is unlikely to change that. Putting another block on top of a shaky pile isn't going to make it stronger, it's going to make it more likely to topple. It's also important to consider how your relationship problems impact your child, or how they may impact your child in the future. Problems that you are able to cope with may have a devastating influence on your child.

There are lots of ways to work out instability and uncertainty in a relationship. If you and your partner communicate well, try talking openly and honestly about your situation and your feelings. Avoiding the subject won't make it go away.

Counseling is an excellent option that helps many couples solve problems in their relationships. You can see a marriage therapist (many "marriage therapists" are actually skilled at helping partners solve problems in their relationships, and the word marriage shouldn't keep you away), a counselor, a social worker, or even a member of the clergy experienced in helping couples work through their issues. There are counselors who specialize in gay/lesbian relationships and others who specialize in heterosexual couples. Get references and ask about specialties or areas of experience.

If you are content and happy with your relationship the way it exists, even if you feel it can be unstable, no one should make you feel that you need to make changes or get assistance. If your arrangement works in your life and works for your child, you have every right to continue with it.

Advocacy Tip ▰▰▰▰▰▰▰▰▰▰▰▰▰▰▰▰▰▰▰▰▰▰▰

Many people still assume that if a heterosexual couple lives together and has children, that they are married. This assumption can only be changed if unmarried couples with children speak out and make their numbers visible. Some couples are very comfortable doing this and believe this is a cause they must pursue. Others are happy to live their lives as their own and let others draw what conclusions they may. You have to make a choice based on what is most comfortable for you.

How to Think about Your Parenting Relationship

Whether you and your partner live in the same household or in different homes, you are both equal partners in your child's life. There are people who may try to make you feel as though one of you is not a "real" parent, as if somehow your unmarried status, choice of partners, or your living arrangement impacts your relationship with your child. This is absolutely not the case. Being a parent has nothing to do with marriage, sexual preferences, or where you live. It is an emotional bond between you and your child, and it is up to you to control that.

It's also important to remember that you and your significant other are parenting partners and that you have the same relationship to each other as other parents do. Again, unmarried status, sexual preference, or living arrangements have no impact on your parenting capabilities. You have chosen to raise a child together, and this means that you will be parenting partners for the rest of your lives. Your relationship to each other is important and real, and other people's opinions can't change that.

👫 Life **Lessons**

Kirsten and Yo-Ming have two children and have been a couple for many years. Before they had children, they didn't think much about the fact that they weren't married. It wasn't something that was important to them. Their relationship worked, and that was all that mattered. Once they had children, it seemed that every time they turned around, the fact that they weren't married was brought up. The receptionist at the pediatrician's office asked Kirsten for "your husband's" social security number. When Kirsten talked to teachers they also referred to him as her husband. She realized that because many married women keep their last names after marriage, teachers simply assumed she had done the same. When they went to events at the school, other parents would talk to Yo-Ming about "your wife." At first this really bothered them. They each felt a need to carefully explain to the person they were speaking to that they were not and had never been married and this was by choice. The response was often a blank stare or a look of confusion. Finally, they just decided to stop wasting their breath. They decided to let other people think whatever they liked.

The children always knew they weren't married and understood their reasons. As they grew older, they had more questions, but it was always something they were able to talk about as a family. They all understood they were a family unit and marriage had nothing to do with that. Once Kirsten and Yo-Ming stopped explaining to other people, they felt a sense of relief and peace. They still hear references to "your husband" or "your wife" but hardly notice them anymore. When they fill out forms, they are always careful to indicate they are not married, but have stopped trying to correct everyone's mistaken impression. The children, however, have taken this up as their cause and always correct people who make this assumption.

Chapter 9

Parents but Not Partners: Parenting as an Unmarried Non-Romantic Couple

If you and your partner have a child together, but are no longer in a romantic relationship with each other, or perhaps never were in a long-term relationship with each other, you need to find a way to parent together, even though you do not wish to share your lives with each other.

Creating a Parenting Relationship

When a child has two parents, it is most beneficial for that child if the parents can find a way to work together. Children need the security of knowing that the two most important people in their lives care about them and care enough to work together.

Although you and the other parent do not wish to be life partners with each other, you will forever be parenting partners, whether you like it or not. You created your child or family together, and you have a responsibility to find a way to work together for the benefit of that child.

When you and your partner break up, or if you decide to have a child together even though you do not plan on being a committed couple, it is essential that you take some time to think about how you will parent together. It's likely that your decision not to be together is one that is emotionally difficult for you, or at least one that required a lot of thought and consideration. This kind of decision or result is not easy for anyone to deal with, so the first thing you must do is not expect too much of yourself. You have issues to work through and emotions to cope with. You are human and you can't simply put what has happened behind you and not feel any effects of it.

Creating a Parenting Relationship after a Breakup

When you and your partner end your relationship with each other, you are likely to be struggling to cope with emotional, financial, and practical issues, in addition to parenting issues. All of these issues are important, and all of them are difficult; however, when dealing with parenting issues, you're dealing not only with the impact on yourself, but on your child.

The first thing you must do is change how you think about your partner. You are no longer lovers, partners, or two parts of a whole. Your partner may be your ex, but he or she is also your child's other parent. Make a mental shift in how you think about your former partner and try to refocus on him or her as your child's parent. You have a parenting relationship together, and the center of that relationship is your child. You can't magically erase all the feelings you have about your ex and all you've gone through, but you can make an effort to focus on the parenting issues when you are together.

When you first break up, it is important to create a temporary plan for how you and your child will get through the next days and weeks. Set up a temporary schedule and try not to think too far ahead. Take small steps for now.

Once you have gotten through the initial separation, you and the other parent need to work together to create a plan that will work for your family for the upcoming months. Later in this chapter we will address how to create a schedule. In addition to a schedule you need to create some rules for yourselves. You're entering a new phase of your relationship together and it can be helpful to work out some ground rules. These can be as simple as agreeing to be respectful and tolerant of each other, or as detailed as working out specific times when you will have phone calls together to discuss parenting or scheduling.

One of the hardest things to deal with is the fact that you cannot completely cut the other parent out of your life. Sometimes after a breakup, completely cutting off all contact seems like a good solution. When you share a child together, though, you must find a way to continue to see each other, communicate, and work together. This means putting aside some of your animosity and focusing instead on making the parenting part of your relationship work. It can be challenging, but it is always well worth the effort.

Creating a Parenting Relationship If You Were Never a Couple

If you and the other parent had a brief time together and were never really a couple, or if you are two friends who have decided you want to have a family together, you must create a shift in how you think about each other now that you have a child. You've chosen to take on the responsibility of a family together, and now you need to find a way to work together to create a good life for your child. You have created a permanent tie to each other, and it can take some time to adjust to the finality of that.

If you and the other parent don't really know each other that well, it can be challenging to work out a parenting relationship because you may feel the other person is still strange to you in some ways. Learning to work cooperatively and make big decisions together is an adjustment. Having some meetings in which you take the time to talk in a neutral way and become more familiar with each other can be helpful. You don't need to become best buddies, but you do need to have a basic understanding of the other parent's schedule, family, living situation, and lifestyle. You also need to talk about what kind of parents you see yourselves being and how you can find a way to allow these two parenting styles to coexist. You need to develop tolerance for each other's differences and learn to see what your child will love in the other person.

Creating some ground rules for your relationship can be helpful. It takes time to build trust if you did not have a previous relationship with each other. It takes a lot of work to be parents together, and doing so without any kind of underlying relationship requires more work and more commitment.

If you and the other parent had a friendship before you became parents, you have a solid basis on which to build a parenting relationship. However, it is important to understand that being parents together is much more challenging, emotional, and difficult than being friends. Suddenly you are forever tied to each other and this wonderful little person. The sense of responsibility is huge, and you may suddenly expect more from each other.

It can also be tempting to imagine you and the other parent becoming romantically involved—after all, that's what happens in movies, you may think. Be realistic about how you feel about each other and relate to each other. These kinds of feelings can result in a lot of hurt if they are not reciprocated, so it is important to be honest, yet careful, with each other's feelings.

Talking over your plans for how you will parent together, communicate, and help each other is essential. It takes time to build a good parenting relationship, even if you liked and trusted each other before.

Deciding on a Residence for Your Child

If you and the other parent will not be living together, you need to make some immediate decisions as to where your child will live. You have three options. The child could reside with you, with your partner, or with both of you. Ideally, your child will have lots of time with both of you and will spend time at both your homes. Some parenting experts believe that sharing the child's time equally (and splitting the child's time between two homes) is the best solution. Other experts disagree. You as a parent need to make a decision that is best for your child and your situation.

There are some situations in which it is necessary to choose one home to be your child's main residence. Some children simply do not do well splitting their time equally between two homes. It may make sense for the child to live at the home closest to the school or to health care providers who provide constant and ongoing care. One parent may have a work schedule that is not as conducive to having the child live at that home. The reasons for choosing a single residence are many, and if that is what works in your situation, that is what you should do.

If you aren't sure where your child should live, think about the two homes and situations. Which home has a room for the child? Which home is closest to school? Which home has a parent there more of the time? Which home is the child most accustomed to? Where is childcare more available? These factors can help you make your decision.

If you and the other parent cannot agree about where your child should live, don't panic. It's normal to feel conflicted about an important decision like this. It does not mean you have to be at each other's throats or immediately run to a court for help. Instead, try sitting down and talking about what life would be like for the child at each home. Compare schedules and lifestyles. If you wish, you could ask an unbiased friend to sit in and talk with both of you. If you still are unable to agree, you could go see a mediator who could help you reach a decision on your own. Remember that if you make a decision and it doesn't work, you can always try something else.

Parenting in the Same Residence

If you and your partner will continue to share a home, you will be able to raise your child together under one roof. Another option, which is becoming more popular, is for your child to stay in place in the home and have the parents alternate their time there. This allows the child to have the stability of one home, while permitting each parent separate parenting time.

Sharing a home with your child has benefits and drawbacks. The obvious benefit is there is no change in environment for the child, which reduces the need for drop-offs, pickups, and the passing back and forth of the child's belongings. It offers more consistency and stability for the child. On the other hand, it increases the potential for parental friction. Not only are you sharing parenting responsibilities, but you are also sharing a physical residence. If you have two very different living styles (such as one person being messy and the other being neat), this can be difficult. If you plan to live in the home at the same time, you may also experience personality clashes.

The key to making a shared residence work is very clear rules. It can help to write them down so there can be no confusion over who is to do the laundry, feed the dog, mow the lawn, and so on. You might also wish to agree to eat several meals together each week as a family and to arrange times when each parent will have private time with the child. It is a good idea to designate private areas of the home, such as individual bedrooms, so that you can each have your privacy. You may also want to establish ground rules about social lives. You may not be comfortable with the other parent bringing dates or love interests to the family home, so you should talk about your expectations.

While a shared residence is a long-term solution for some families, for many others it is something that works best in the first few years of the child's life. It often functions as a transition for a couple that has broken up and allows the child and parents the time to adjust to the change in family structure and gradually move apart.

Creating a Parenting Schedule

The primary consideration in creating a parenting schedule should be your child's needs. A parenting schedule should not be about the convenience of the parents. The entire point of a parenting schedule is to allow the child time with both parents and to encourage a healthy relationship with both parents. A parenting schedule is not about one parent winning and the other losing. It is not a way to punish each other or control each other. When courts make decisions about parenting schedules, they rely on what is called the best-interests rule. This means that they make their decisions based on what is in that particular child's best interest, in those circumstances. There is no presumption that a mother or father makes a better parent. The court decides by looking at the situation and considering what would work best for the child. When you are considering scheduling your parenting times, you should try to apply the same rule when possible.

Your Child's Needs

Once you have determined where the child will live, you can focus on creating a schedule that allows you to share time with the child. First you need to consider your child's needs. If your child is school age, transporting back and forth between homes for weeknight overnights may not work. If your child has a busy sports or activities schedule, you should take this into consideration. Some children have emotional or developmental needs that make it difficult for them to transition between parents often, so this is another consideration. Teenagers who have established friends, jobs, and social lives need to be able to live their own lives to some extent, and providing them the freedom to do that is another important consideration.

You will also find that your child's needs change as he or she grows. It may be easy to transport a toddler back and forth a few times a week, but a school-age child may have a harder time with that kind of schedule. And while a set weekly schedule may work well during elementary school years, a teen may need more flexibility and control of the situation.

There is no one-size-fits-all parenting plan. Each family should make its own decision based on the particular needs of that child and the circumstances of those parents. Evaluate your plan by looking at whether it offers your child enough time with both parents and is comfortable for the child.

Creating the Schedule

The thought of creating a schedule with the other parent may feel overwhelming at first, but the two of you need to sit down with your calendars and try to come up with something that will work for everyone. Compare your schedule, the other parent's schedule, and your child's schedule, then try to make a rough draft for how the next month should look. Look for a pattern to emerge. It makes sense to try to create a regular weekly or monthly schedule. This makes it easy for everyone to remember, and it also gives your child something solid to rely on ("I always see Dad on Sundays," for example).

Many parents rely on the traditional "one night a week and every other weekend" plan that is commonly ordered by family courts. The nonresidential parent spends one evening a week with the child and then has the child overnight (usually two nights—Friday and Saturday) on alternate weekends.

This traditional plan might be something you want to consider, but that doesn't necessarily mean it is what you should choose to do. Whenever possible, try to think creatively about your parenting plan. If one parent always has Mondays off, the child could spend every Sunday night there and that parent could take the child to school and pick him or her up afterward. If one parent works until 2 P.M. each day, the child could go to that parent's home every day after school. You need to think about everyone's availability and then try to maximize it. While it might look great on paper to have your child at your home every weekday, in reality if your child is home with a sitter while you're working until 8 P.M. each night, the child is not getting the benefit of parental time with that kind of schedule.

Factors to Consider When Creating a Parenting Schedule

- Your schedule

- The other parent's schedule

- Where you each will be living and how far apart the homes are

- Your child's school and homework schedule

- Your child's activities and sports schedule

- Any health conditions or special needs your child might have

- Your child's sleep schedule

- Your child's homework responsibilities

- Cost and availability of daycare and babysitting

Don't create a schedule that is not going to be practical. For example, if you know you can't reasonably get out of work before 6 P.M., don't agree to pick up your child at 5:30 P.M. every Friday.

Once you've worked out a schedule, make sure you and the other parent write it down. It is also important to share it with your child. Young children can benefit from color-coded calendars—red for days with Mom and blue for days with Dad, for example. Older children can write the information on their own calendars or put it in their PDA.

Holidays

In addition to your schedule of daily life, you will probably want to create a holiday and vacation schedule. The first thing you will need to do is create a list of holidays you want to share with your child. You may want to include some of the following:

- Hanukkah

- Christmas Day

- Christmas Eve

- New Year's Day

- Valentine's Day

- Easter

- Passover

- Memorial Day

- Mother's Day

- Father's Day

- Your child's birthday

- Your birthday

- The other parent's birthday

- Fourth of July

- Labor Day

- Rosh Hashanah

- Yom Kippur

- Halloween

- Thanksgiving

- Other days off from school

Some parents choose to alternate holidays (I get Thanksgiving this year, you get it next year, or I get Christmas Eve, you get Christmas Day, I get New Year's, and so on), while others choose to create a set schedule that will be the same every year. When you are working out a holiday schedule, think creatively. You can split a day into two parts, celebrate something the day after the traditional holiday, and even spend some holidays all together as a family. And what works for you this year might not be what will work next year, so be sure to keep an open mind. Remember each family's traditions. If your family celebrates on Christmas Eve, it may make sense for you to plan to have your child that day and the other parent to have Christmas Day every year.

In addition to holidays, you will also want to plan how you will share your child's vacation time. One of you may want to take a trip with your child during school vacation. Some parents like to split up summertime in weekly blocks. It's also common for parents who don't see their children very often during the school year to spend extended time with the child over the summer. Create a summer plan that works for you and your child.

Small Details

Once you've worked out the schedule, you might think you're done. There are actually some other smaller decisions to be made. And surprisingly, these small details are often the ones that cause the most problems, so take some time now to work through them and come to an agreement.

- Transportation. Will the person with the child be the one responsible for taking the child to the other parent, or will the parent who is waiting for the child come and get him or her?

- Tardiness. How big of a window will you give each other for lateness? Will you automatically allow half an hour? Will you expect a phone call if the other person will be more than fifteen minutes late?

- Entering homes. Will you come into each other's home or exchange your child on the doorstep, in the driveway, or on the sidewalk?

- Illness. If your child is home sick from school, does the parenting plan change? How sick is too sick to go to the other parent's home? Consider some of these situations in advance so they don't come as a surprise to either of you.

- Laundry. Who will wash the clothing the child wears when at the different homes? Will it be returned at the end of that visit or the next visit?

- Forgotten items. If your child leaves an essential item (anything from a pacifier to homework to a cell phone, depending on the age) at the other home, how will you get it back to the child and who will drive it?

- Phone calls. Most parents agree that their child can have phone contact with both parents, but you don't want the other parent calling every hour during your time. How much is too much?

- Schedule changes. If one of you needs to make changes to the schedule how much notice do you need to give each other? How often can you make changes?

- Activities. Will parenting time interfere with your child's activities? If a child wants to plan an activity during one parent's time, does the child need to get explicit permission from that parent? Do you need to consult each other before signing a child up for a long-term activity that will impact both of your times?

- Meals. If a pickup/drop-off is scheduled near a mealtime, clarify where the child will be eating so you can avoid one parent preparing a meal and being disappointed to find the child has already eaten. With younger children, will you communicate with each other how much the child has eaten or drunk while with you?

- Rules. Will you have the same bedtime at both homes? What kinds of rules will you both use about homework, chores, or appropriate language? Rules don't have to be exactly the same, but some consistency makes it easier for everyone involved, especially for your child.

- Visits with friends. Will your child be able to have friends over and go to friends' houses while at each of your homes?

Planning Ahead

Once you work out a parenting schedule, it will feel like a great relief to have that aspect of your life settled. However, what works for your family today may not work next year or the year after. Children grow and change, parents move, get married, and get new jobs. There are many factors that may pop up in the coming years that could necessitate changes to your parenting plan. The best thing you can do is try to remain flexible. It can be helpful to sit down with the other parent once or twice a year and review how things are going. Talk about what's working or isn't working. Discuss upcoming changes and possible ways to manage them. Anticipating change and planning ahead for it is much better than waiting for changes to happen and then scrambling to react to them.

Formalizing Your Plan

Once you've worked out the details of your parenting plan, you need to decide if you want to have the plan recognized by the court. There are benefits and drawbacks. If you do get a court order, then you have something final in writing that everyone has to follow. If there is a major violation of the agreement, you have a legal mechanism that will deal with it. Having a formal court order can also make things easier when dealing with schools. However, going to court can be very stressful and feel very confrontational. Some people feel it is invasive. It can also be costly if you go to court and air all your grievances and battle every last detail out.

Advocacy Tip

Too often people see family courts as mechanisms that decide their fate for them. Instead, families need to take control of their own lives and the choices available to them. There is no reason to go ask a judge to create a plan for your family if you can possibly create one yourselves. A court-created plan should be for high-conflict families. Other families can learn to solve their own problems. You and the other parent can meet and talk, have a friend help you, or go see a mediator while creating a parenting plan. Once you reach an agreement, it is very easy to open a court proceeding and submit a stipulation at the same time without a protracted hearing or contentious process. The court will then issue an order with the terms of your agreement. You get the best of both worlds—a custom-made agreement and a legal court order.

One common misconception about court orders is that people think you have to go back to court every time you want to make an adjustment to the schedule. This is not true at all, and in fact most parenting orders contain a clause that authorizes parents to make changes to it when they agree. Judges do not want you to come back through that revolving door to make changes you both agree to. The goal of family court is to try to make families self-sufficient.

Working Out Problems with Parenting

You and the other parent are two different people, with different views and opinions. You are not a couple, and it is to be expected that you are not going to agree all of the time. You're going to rub each other the wrong way, make decisions the other person disagrees with, and sometimes hurt or upset each other. You're both human, and you both need to make an effort to be understanding, flexible, and forgiving.

Try to let the small things go, if possible. If you jump on everything the other person does that you don't agree with or don't like, you could spend all day, every day, arguing. Try to look at the big picture. If your child is loved, safe, and well cared for, and there is nothing terribly wrong, maybe you're better off not rocking the boat if you can help it.

When you encounter major disagreements with the other parent, try to stay calm. It is easy to get emotional about you child, but you need to try very hard to approach the situation in a reasonable and calm way. Try to find a compromise as a solution for your disagreement. Focus on the problem at hand—not on previous transgressions by the other person, emotional scars from your relationship, or your own life stressors. Always try to focus on what would be best for your child.

If your child is in danger, is exposed to unsafe conditions, or is not being cared for properly, then you absolutely must stand your ground and protect your child.

Talking to Your Child about Your Relationship

No matter what kind of an arrangement you and the other parent have, your child is bound to have questions. Whether you were together and have split up, were never together, or decided to have children together as friends, your child will have natural curiosity about the situation and will compare it to other parents.

Let your child's questions be your guide as to how complete your answers need to be. Many children want to know why their parents broke up, and often the unasked but underlying question is "Was it my fault?" You want to be certain to reassure your child that he or she had nothing to do with the decision you made about your relationship.

No matter what your living arrangements are, you will want to stress to your child that you are all a family and always will be. It is common for children of parents who are divorced or no longer together as a couple to hope and dream that someday their parents will get married or become a couple. It's important to be clear with your child that this won't happen.

👫 Life **Lessons**

Laurie and Keith had a one-night stand, and their daughter Kendra was the result. Because they never really dated or got to know each other, there were some difficult times after Laurie discovered she was pregnant, told Keith, and decided to have the baby. Keith felt trapped, and Laurie felt rejected. It took several months for them to find their way back to being civil and reasonable with each other.

Before Kendra was born, Laurie and Keith tried to talk about how they would parent together, but because neither of them had any children, they didn't feel as though they really knew what to expect. They did agree that the baby would live with Laurie—she was going to move in with her mother and it seemed like the best solution. Keith really wanted to be a father to the baby, but was a little scared about being a father. They didn't reach any agreement about a parenting schedule and decided to wait and see.

Keith was with Laurie when Kendra was born, and they were both shocked and amazed by the life they had created. Keith signed an acknowledgment of paternity. Laurie came home from the hospital, and Keith came over every day. Together they learned about their daughter. Soon Keith's workload became heavy and he didn't have as much time available. His visits dropped off. Laurie began to think it wasn't fair that he wasn't showing up, and she also started to think he ought to help her financially. When Keith did come to see the baby, Laurie was cold to him and made things difficult.

This made him angry. After a month or so, Keith started to think that he would like to be able to bring his daughter to his own apartment. Laurie completely rejected the idea of the baby being with him out of her sight. She was sure he wasn't competent and vowed it would never happen.

Laurie and Keith stopped talking, but Keith did not give up on his daughter. He went to court and filed papers for custody. Laurie was outraged that he could possibly think he could take their baby away from her. Tensions were high, and it looked as though there was going to be a full-on custody battle. However, Laurie's mom had been talking to Keith's mom, and both grandmothers agreed that it was terrible to see their grandbaby's parents acting so immature. They got the parents together and insisted that they find a way to work it out. Laurie's mom explained to Keith how Laurie had been feeling, and Keith's mom explained to Laurie how Keith had been feeling. They had never really thought about how the other parent was feeling. The grandmothers made some suggestions about how they could handle the situation.

They met a few more times, and with the help of the grandmothers, Laurie and Keith agreed to see a counselor together to help them learn to develop a parenting relationship. The counselor talked to them about communicating, developing trust, and forming a family for their daughter. They were able to work out a parenting schedule that gave them both time with the baby. Kendra spends three nights a week with Keith and four nights with Laurie. Keith is able to continue with his workload and Laurie has gone back to school. They got the agreement formalized in court and also worked out a child support plan. They still have differences and have moments where they do not understand or like the other person, but they have reached a point in their relationship where they respect each other and find a way to work with the other person because they believe it is what is best for their daughter.

Chapter 10

Solo Parenting: Parenting as an Unmarried Single

According to the U.S. Census, single-parent families account for 27 percent of the homes with children under age eighteen. The number of single-parent homes continues to rise every year. Whether you are a single unmarried parent by choice or by circumstances, you are by no means alone. While there used to be a stigma associated with unmarried single people raising children, this type of family has gained lots of acceptance in recent years, partly because of celebrities raising children alone, but also because more people are meeting families just like yours in their own communities.

Coping with How You Got Here

Whether you are pregnant, a new parent, or have been parenting for years, it can sometimes be difficult to work through the situation that brought you to where you are today. Single parenting is not an easy job, although you most likely know by now that it is the most rewarding one you will ever have.

Loving Your Choice

If you chose to become a single parent and did not want another parent involved or did not have any other way to become a parent, you may have used a donor, surrogate, or adoption. You have woken up every day knowing who you are and that you want to be your child's family. It's likely that you have encountered or will encounter people with inappropriate questions: Where's the dad/mom? What country is your child from? Why isn't there another parent? Why would you do this alone? Don't you know children need two parents? Although these questions are hard to adjust to in the beginning, they do get easier to deal with.

You made a decision based on love—the love you have to give and the love your child deserved. While choosing to become a parent on your own is still considered to be out of the ordinary, the fact is more and more people, women in particular, are choosing this option. There is no reason you should not be proud of the choice you made. Deciding to become a solo parent is one many people would be afraid to make.

Loving Your Circumstances

If you became a single parent by circumstance—the other parent completely checked out of your and your child's life or you needed to leave for whatever reason—you may still be dealing with feelings of abandonment, anger, resentment, and grief. These feelings are very real and important. If you need help, find a therapist who can help you cope with them. A therapist is just another piece of the support system that many parents rely on.

Despite how you may feel about your child's other parent, you are most likely filled with joy about being a parent. Others you talk to may say things such as they can't imagine how difficult it must be and they don't know how you do it. It can be frustrating to always hear such remarks when in fact you love being a parent and raising your child and don't want or need sympathy. People mean well but may not understand what your life is truly like.

Although all single parents face challenges and difficult times, it is important to be grateful for what you do have in your life. The other parent's loss is your gain. The circumstances with the other parent are what have brought you to the place you are today—the wonderful position of being the parent of a child you adore.

Organizing Your Life as a Solo Parent

Single parents have some considerations other parents do not have. Since you are your child's only parent, you need to make some decisions and put some safeguards into place to protect your child should something happen to you. It's never any fun to think about "what ifs," but as a single parent, it is the responsible thing to do. You also have to make decisions about things such as childcare and your career path that will affect both you and your child.

Will and Guardian

A will is a very important document for a single parent to have. Most people think of wills as documents that divide their belongings after their death. This is an important feature of a will, but as a single parent, your child would be your sole heir under state intestacy law (laws that decide how to divide the belongings of people who do not have wills) and would get everything anyhow. As a single parent, a will is crucial for you because it allows you to name a guardian for your child, should you pass away while he or she is a minor.

If you do not name a guardian in your will, your state probate or family court would be left to make the decision. Most parents want to have control over this decision, and the only way to do so is to have a will made that names a guardian.

When thinking about who you would like as a guardian, consider your close friends and family. Think about the people who share the same values that you do and those who already have a strong relationship with your child. It is important to talk with the person or persons (some people choose to name a married couple as joint guardians) you are considering to find out if this is a responsibility they would be willing to accept. You should also name an alternate guardian, in case your first choice is unable to take on the responsibility at the time of your death. It's important to understand that a guardian is different from a godparent. Even if you name a godparent in a religious ceremony, he or she has no legal right to become your child's guardian. Also, keep in mind that you have the option of naming a separate guardian to be in charge of your child's financial affairs.

It is important that you have an attorney draw up your will to be sure that the wording in it fits your state requirements and that the execution (signing and witnessing) also complies with the requirements of your state. Information on the various state requirements is available at *www .livingtrustnetwork.com/content/lwt/applicable_state_laws/requirements_ for_wills/index.php*. Writing a will on your own is not a good idea. It is possible to have a simple will drawn up for a few hundred dollars, and this should be a priority for you as a single parent. It may be difficult to bring yourself to think about the questions involved, but once you have the will completed, you will feel a sense of relief and completion.

Career

As a solo parent, you are the single provider in your household. When you're a single person on your own, this can be fun and exciting, but when you are a single parent, it can feel like a heavy weight at times because you know that not only must you provide for yourself, but for your child as well.

Gone are the days when a single mother or father raising a child alone was a kind of stigma in the workplace. Many employers are understanding and accommodating because so many people are single (albeit often divorced) parents. But single parents do not constitute a protected group for the purposes of employment discrimination laws (however, a pregnancy discrimination law protects pregnant women; see *www.eeoc.gov/facts/fs-preg.html*), and there are still many people who believe they are "mommy-tracked" (treated differently and given less responsibility) after becoming a parent.

If you need to take time off from work when your child enters your family, you may be eligible to do so under the federal Family and Medical Leave Act (FMLA), which allows new parents to take time off from work without pay and guarantees a job will still be waiting when they return. There are restrictions on the law: Your employer must have at least fifty employees, certain top employees do not receive the same guarantees, you have to work there for a certain period of time before you are eligible, and you may only have an equivalent job waiting for you when you return. For more information about FMLA, see *www .dol.gov/esa/whd/fmla*. Some states also have their own family-leave laws. Family leave can give a new parent the time needed to adjust to the changes a child brings.

When considering how to manage your job and be a parent, there are some creative options to consider. Your employer might be open to you telecommuting or working from home part of the week. You might be able to take advantage of flex time, which allows you to work the same number of hours but in a flexible way that allows you to adjust the schedule to your needs. Some employers have on-site daycare, which can be a lifesaver for a single parent.

Childcare

Childcare is an important aspect of any single parent's life. Every single parent needs reliable childcare assistance at some point. The good news is there are many wonderful options available to you and your child. You may use a childcare center; employ a nanny, au pair, or sitter at your home; take your child to an in-home childcare; or rely on a friend or relative for childcare.

Whatever option you choose, it is important that you feel completely comfortable with the person or center. Ask for references, read any contract carefully, discuss rates, make unscheduled drop-ins, ask questions about safety and sanitary procedures, and get information about insurance and licenses. For a checklist of questions, visit *www .naccrra.org/docs/parent/38IndicatorsChecklist.pdf*.

Depending on the type of childcare provider you use, you may wish to sign a consent to obtain medical care (see Appendix A), which would allow the childcare provider to get emergency medical care for your child if you can't be reached.

When working with a childcare center, consider whether you want to authorize other people (friends or family) to pick up your child from childcare. Centers usually require written authorization from you in advance, and you never know when something could come up that would require you to have someone else pick your child up.

Another important consideration for childcare is a backup plan. Most daycare centers have health policies that ask you not to bring your child when he or she is sick, and unfortunately, young children do get sick often. Creating a backup plan that relies on a friend or relative or that gives you access to a paid sitter who can come to your home can be a lifesaver.

School

Although schools are accustomed to working with single-parent families (most of which are divorced), there are still some considerations to take into account. When completing paperwork for school, be sure to provide all your numbers—home, cell, office, and so on—so that you can be reached when needed. It may make sense to provide an alternate number of a friend or relative to contact in emergencies if you can't be reached. You may wish to authorize that same person to pick your child up from school from regular dismissal and also if your child is sent home sick.

Since schools and preschools regularly have children prepare Mother's Day and Father's Day cards and gifts, you may wish to speak to your child's teacher and alert him or her to the fact that the child does not have one of those parents. Some teachers make it an optional activity or suggest that children without that parent make a card or gift for a grandparent, aunt/uncle, or special family friend (although this still highlights the fact that the child is "missing" a parent). If you're uncomfortable with that idea, you could arrange to take your child out of school during the times the class will be working on that project. That's a personal choice, just as it is with parents who remove kids from Halloween activities because it clashes with their religious beliefs. As a parent, you have to decide what you are most comfortable with.

If you need childcare after school, find out if your child's school has an in-building, after-school program, or whether any area after-school programs transport children from your school. An after-school program can bridge the gap between the end of the school day and the end of a parent's workday. If there are no after-school programs available, consider talking to some area at-home parents who might be interested in providing after-school care for your child.

Life Insurance

Life insurance can offer protection for your child should something happen to you. Not only does life insurance offer protection for a minor child, but it can also provide a financial cushion for a young adult child of a single parent. Experts are divided about the value of life insurance. Some financial advisors suggest it is better to take the money you would spend on life insurance premiums and invest it instead. This makes the money accessible to you at any point should you want to buy a house or pay for college, and it may ultimately offer a better return. However, taking out a life insurance policy means a set sum of money will be paid to your child should something happen to you, and it is available immediately. It could take years to build up that amount of money through investments. Some experts recommend doing both—setting up investments and also buying life insurance, so that you can have the best of both options.

If you do decide to purchase life insurance, experts recommend purchasing enough to cover five to ten times your annual income. Another way to think about it is to purchase enough for your child to live on until adulthood, so if your child is two years old, you might want to buy enough to cover sixteen years. Note, however, that if something were to happen to you, your child's financial guardian could invest the life insurance payout and increase the value of it that way.

Online Single-Parent Resources

- Making Lemonade *www.makinglemonade.com*

- Single Rose *www.singlerose.com*

- Single Parents Network *www.singleparentsnetwork.com*

- Single Mothers by Choice *www.singlemothersbychoice.com*

- Single Mothers *www.singlemothers.org*

- Single Moms *www.singlemoms.com*

- Solo Mother *www.solomother.com*

There are two basic types of life insurance: term insurance and cash value life insurance. A term insurance policy exists for a set number of years and pays out a fixed amount on your death. You pay a premium each year to keep the policy alive. Cash value insurance provides life insurance, but has a cash value available to you as well. The money you invest in the account earns interest. The interest accumulates, or you can use it to pay the yearly premium. This type of insurance is really a combination of term insurance and an investment.

You may already have life insurance through your employer, credit union, AAA, or credit card. Check existing policies and make your child your beneficiary on all of them. Life insurance exists outside your will—you can't affect the beneficiary of your life insurance policies by naming beneficiaries in your will. You need to contact the insurance companies directly and complete their paperwork to change insurance beneficiaries. It's also important to remember to do this after you add children to your family. If you have one child and list him or her as your life insurance beneficiary, but then have a second child and forget to change the policy, should you die, the money belongs only to the first child.

If you are looking to buy a new life insurance policy, do not do so when you are pregnant if you can avoid it. Your risk of death is actually increased while pregnant, so it would cost more to buy a policy at this point.

Be sure to comparison shop. Most states have laws that require companies to provide you with information that makes comparing policies easy. Ask for a net payment index, which can help make comparing easier. Also be sure to ask about the surrender cost index, which shows how the value of the policy will grow.

Disability Insurance

Disability is the insurance that most people don't think about, but it is something a single parent definitely should have. In fact, for most of your life, you're more likely to become disabled than you are to die, so disability insurance is arguably more important than life insurance.

Disability insurance guarantees you a monthly income should you become temporarily or permanently disabled and unable to work. Some states have state-run disability programs, and some employers voluntarily purchase these policies for their employees. Social Security Disability is not enough for anyone to rely on and is meant to only provide basic subsistence living.

Advocacy Tip

If you give birth to a child and the father has chosen not to be involved, or you have decided you don't wish to involve him at all, leaving the father section part of the birth certificate blank may make things easier for you. If you do complete this section, whenever you show your child's birth certificate (such as for school registration and so on) you will have to explain why he is not involved, and you may be asked if you have a custody order. Leaving the certificate blank leaves the father completely out of the picture and reduces the questions involved.

Find out if you are covered by a state or company plan. If you are, learn how much the benefits are. Usually these benefits pay just a fraction of your monthly income at the time of disability. Purchasing a policy yourself can provide peace of mind and a sense of security for you and your child.

Disability insurance policies generally have a waiting period before they kick in. Once they do kick in, they usually do not cover more than 60 to 70 percent of your income. No one gets rich living off a disability policy, but it can offer security, especially when you combine federal, state, and private policy payments. Look for a policy that cannot be cancelled and is guaranteed to be renewable. A policy that guarantees a cost-of-living adjustment is also worth considering. A policy that provides coverage for disability resulting from accidents and injuries offers the most extensive coverage.

Getting Support and Backup

When you first considered raising a child alone, you may have felt overwhelmed or a bit daunted at the prospect. Our culture often places a heavy emphasis on the importance of two-parent homes, when really the key to being a parent is to have other people you can count on to help you, support you, and be involved in your family.

The thing to remember is that no one truly does it alone, and relying on other people is how we all survive. Being part of a family, group of friends, and community helps you in all aspects of your life, including parenting.

Family

If you're close to your family, they can be an excellent resource for you and your child. Grandparents not only enrich a child's life through love and attention, but also can offer parents much-needed help. Simply knowing you can pick up the phone and call your mom or your brother to come over and help when you and your child have the flu or when you desperately need just a few moments to yourself can mean the world.

If your family is able to help you, it can make you feel you are part of a larger entity—you're not just a parent and child making your way through the world, you are part of a family that sticks together and helps each other. Having that kind of support and encouragement makes everything easier.

If you aren't close to your family, the thing to remember is there are many kinds of families. Many people form families with people who are not blood relatives. A family is any group of people you can rely on.

It's not uncommon for some families to disapprove when a person makes a decision to become a solo parent. Dealing with that kind of disapproval can be devastating, even when you are in the midst of the overwhelming joy of becoming a parent. Some families do eventually see the errors of their ways and open their hearts to their grandchild, so change is always possible.

Friends

Friends that you love and rely on are irreplaceable when you are parenting alone. A circle of friends who support you and are there to help you can make you feel understood, respected, and involved. Friends sometimes offer support that family can't and may play important roles in your child's life as honorary aunts, uncles, or godparents.

Friends who are parents can provide an important support group, and can be there to offer advice, to give tips, and to commiserate as you raise your children. They can provide gatherings where parents and kids can connect and have fun. Some single parents specifically join single-parent support groups to meet up with other solo parents so that they can share the particular challenges that solo parents face.

Single friends are important too. They might want to dote on your child and buy inappropriate gifts, but they're also good for babysitting. And they are definitely good for helping you remember that you are, in fact, still a single person who has a life outside of being a parent.

Community

Your community is an important part of your support system. Community can consist of a wide range of things such as school, daycare, library, church or temple, neighbors, your pediatrician, extracurricular activities, coworkers—even the little old lady who always stops to say hello to your little one in the park. All around you are people who believe in supporting and strengthening the lives of those who live and work in the community or neighborhood.

Think of your community as a resource where you can turn to have needs met and to meet new people. For example, you may think of your library as a place to pick up books and videos, but it probably also offers toddler or preschool story times, has a children's room or play area, and is most likely populated with other parents and kids who could become acquaintances or friends. A library is also a source of parenting advice and medical information as well as a good place to find an entertaining book for your own pleasure or an animated movie for your child.

There are places and groups all throughout your community that offer information, services, support, potential friends, and more. Schools have bulletin boards where parents can post notices of support groups, churches plan outings to enriching and fulfilling places, local gyms are filled with new parents during the day who are happy to use the on-site daycare, the park can be a magnet for parents looking for other parents, and so on. The resources available to you through your community are astounding, but you need to train yourself to open your eyes and look for the opportunities they afford you and consider the options they offer.

Talking to Your Child about Your Family

Many children are raised in homes with only one parent. The majority of these are children whose parents have divorced, and while they may live with one parent, they have another parent who is active in their life. It will be normal for your child to question why he or she has only one parent. As always, let your child's questions guide your answers. Whether you are explaining an adoption, insemination, or other parent who has chosen not to participate, offer age-appropriate answers. Emphasize the family that your child does have. Talk about the different types of families and family units there are and help your child understand the diversity that exists in families. Emphasize the love and support that exists in your family, extended family, and circle of friends.

👫 Life **Lessons**

Lydia had always dreamed of being a mother. She adored children and couldn't wait to raise her own family. There was only one small problem. She was thirty-nine and had yet to meet the man of her dreams. She and her single girlfriends talked about the problems they faced as single, aging career women. They all wanted to find that perfect guy someday, but so far none of them had. Lydia went to a sperm bank and got some information about insemination and choosing a donor. She thought about it a long time and finally decided she was tired of waiting and was ready to start her family. She confided in her best friend Tomas, who was a gay man in a committed relationship.

Tomas was very supportive of her decision and went with her to her meetings at the sperm bank and held her hand through the insemination. Lydia was overjoyed to find out she was pregnant. Her parents were a bit shocked at the news, and her girlfriends acted supportive but seemed a bit spooked that she would soon be home with a baby instead of out with them at night.

Lydia was a successful graphic artist who had moved up the ladder quickly in her ad agency. She was concerned about her career being affected by her new role as a parent. She was able to arrange a schedule that allowed her to work from home one and a half days per week. She hired a nanny who would care for the baby in her apartment.

Once the baby was born, Lydia's parents fell in love with him, and although they still did not approve of how he came into the world, they couldn't get enough of him and offered to baby-sit at night or on the weekends. Lydia's girlfriends made her promise to go out with them at least once a month. They all doted on her son and wanted to be honorary aunts.

Tomas was the greatest help to Lydia. He came and stayed with her the week after she came home from the birthing center. He and his partner wanted to be very involved in the baby's life and considered themselves to be father figures for him.

Lydia joined a Saturday-morning play group that was made up of many working moms like herself, with a few who were also single parents. Lydia took the baby everywhere with her and enjoyed the interactions with clerks and people on the street. Having the baby caused her to slow down a bit, and she became more familiar with her own neighborhood and the people in it who all seemed to recognize her.

There were still difficult times. The nanny got sick, and Lydia had to scramble for a sitter. There were many nights when she did not get enough sleep. She worried about not paying enough attention to her job and about not spending enough time with her baby. She had no idea how she was going to afford college. She still hoped to meet a man and felt a little left out when one of her friends got married. But despite all this, Lydia adored her son, loved her life, and felt like she had a nearly perfect situation.

Chapter 11
Unmarried Stepparents

If you and your child's other parent are not a couple, there is a very real possibility that one or both of you will at some point find a partner. Your child will then have a stepparent. Many children live in families with stepparents, stepsiblings, and half siblings, and it has become a common family structure.

What Is an Unmarried Stepparent?

When a single person with a child marries, the new spouse becomes the child's stepparent. However, it's becoming more and more common for people to partner without marrying. Some people who have been divorced before feel that they don't want to enter into another marriage. Others have never been married and see no reason to.

When you partner with someone and enter into a committed relationship but do not marry, it may be confusing for your child. One important aspect your child may wonder about is how permanent the relationship is. Children understand that marriage is a permanent (or is supposed to be a permanent) situation, but they may not view a partner moving into the home as a permanent arrangement. If your child is six years old or older, it's important to talk to him or her about what your intentions are. You may need to explain how you feel about each other and how you plan to stay together. Your child may want to know why the partner is moving into the family's home (if that is the arrangement).

It is also likely your child will have questions about what role the partner will play in his or her life. "Can he tell me what to do?" "Do I have to listen to her?" "Why do I have to stay with her when you're at work?" and other such questions are natural. Sometimes it's easy to feel defensive when faced with these kinds of tough questions, but remember, your child is just trying to figure out what is happening and how it will affect him or her. Try to approach these questions with empathy and understanding when possible.

When you become a partner in a long-term, committed relationship, your new partner assumes an important stepparent role in your child's life. Whether you want to refer to the partner as a stepparent is your choice. Using that word may make the situation easier for the child to understand and accept, and may give the child a way to explain the situation to others.

Introducing a New Partner to Your Child

It is normal and healthy to date as a single parent. You need to have a social life and have every right to seek out a mate. Parents are allowed to find personal happiness! Children whose parents are no longer together sometimes are conflicted about seeing a parent dating. It's normal for children to be suspicious of or unfriendly to the people you date. They may view the dates as interlopers into the family or people trying to replace the other parent. Although children do not get to decide whom or how often you date, it is reasonable to take into account your child's feelings. Spending every weekend night away from your child on dates is not the healthiest of choices. Bringing an ever-increasing number of dates to your home may also not be the best choice. Finding a way to balance your personal and parenting lives can be challenging, but it is worth the effort.

When you meet someone you are serious about, it is important to introduce him or her to your child. Expect your child to be ambivalent about the person, even if you have always been a single parent and there is no other parent in the picture to whom the child is trying to be loyal. Gradually introducing an important person in your life to your child takes patience. You cannot expect your child to immediately accept and like this seeming intruder, and sometimes you may encounter outright hostility. The best plan is to take things slow and keep things low-key. Let them get to know each other on their own terms and in their own way. You can't micromanage their relationship or their feelings for each other. They need to be able to develop naturally, over time. Remember that it took you time to get to know and love your partner, and you can't expect your child to feel the same way overnight.

Child-stepparent relationships don't just happen. They have to be built, and it is not easy. Initially, it is a good idea to arrange some family activities, such as a picnic, and have your child and the new partner do some things together within that larger setting. For example, if the child is of preschool age, the two of them might play on the swings together, with the partner pushing the child. It is through mutually shared activities that relationships develop, so it's only smart to plan for some specific relationship building activities between your child and your new partner.

If you make the decision that you want to live with your new partner, expect your child to need time to adjust to this concept. If it has always been just you and your child, adding a new person to the equation can be rocky. If there is another parent, your child may try to be loyal to that other parent by rejecting your new partner. Either way, having someone new move into the home (or moving into the home of your new partner) can feel disruptive and scary to a child. Everyone in the house will need to learn what the boundaries are and how to live with each other.

It takes time for your child to develop a relationship with your new partner and to come to think of him or her as a stepparent. You can't rush this and you can't force it. Emotional bonds have to develop on their own. You can, however, create rules and expectations for how the child will treat the new stepparent. Children should not be allowed to be disrespectful or rude to adults living in the same home with them, even if they don't like them. By setting up what the expectations are, your child will have some guidelines to follow that will help him or her understand how to behave toward the stepparent.

Respecting the Other Parent

If your child has another legal parent, adding a stepparent to the mix can cause concerns for that parent as well. If your child lives primarily with you, the child will most likely see the stepparent more than the other parent simply because of scheduling. It's important to let the other parent know that the stepparent is not in any way taking that parent's place. Parents in this situation want to be assured that they still have an important role in the child's life and that the new family that is being formed will not exclude the child from the parent's life. It's very important that the parenting schedule continue to be honored. Parents worry they will be replaced by the stepparent, and it is important to provide reassurance that this will not happen. Even if you dislike the other parent, it is not healthy to try to encourage your child to replace him or her with a stepparent. That parent-child relationship belongs to the two of them, and you should not try to interfere with it.

The best-case scenario is that you three adults can learn to respect and support each other as you all play a role in raising your child. This isn't always possible, however. Sometimes there is animosity between the other parent and the stepparent; other times there are feelings of resentment or anger over the entire situation. Recognizing that you may not always agree but that your child is important to all of you can help ease tensions. Continuing the parenting schedule is very important for everyone involved. Speaking respectfully about the other parent in front of the child is also key. Making it clear to both child and parent that the stepparent is in no way a replacement for the other parent is helpful. Being patient is the best thing you can do. What seems impossible today is likely to be manageable and more settled in a few months time.

Names

When there is a new stepparent in a child's life, the child has most likely known that person for a period of time while the parent and stepparent were dating. During this period of time the child probably called the stepparent by a first name or perhaps Mr. or Miss with the last name. Once the stepparent becomes part of the home, or after an emotional bond has developed, some families develop other forms of address.

Many children continue to call the stepparent by his or her first name, and if this is comfortable for everyone in your house, it can be a good solution. Less common, but still an option, is to come up with a special name for the stepparent. It is essential that you never allow the child to call the stepparent by the same name as the other parent. For example, if the other parent is Dad or Mommy, your child should never call the stepparent by that same name. Not only is it confusing, but it is also hurtful to the other parent. Some families come up with alternatives. If the other parent is called Daddy, the child might eventually call the stepparent Pop, Baba, or Da. Letting the child choose what to call the stepparent is important. If you try to force something, it won't feel natural and your child will resent it. Talk to your child about what he or she feels comfortable with. If there are other children in the home (stepsiblings or half siblings) it might be natural for the child to eventually refer to the stepparent using the same name the other children in the home use.

If your child has never had another parent, you should use your judgment about what the child should call the stepparent. This is likely something that will evolve over time as they become closer.

When You Are a Stepparent

If you are in the position of being a stepparent to the child of your unmarried partner, you may struggle with what your relationship is supposed to be. You can't suddenly feel like a parent, and you can't suddenly expect the child to see you as one. It takes time to develop a relationship with each other. The best way to start off is simply to try to find common ground and be aware of how the child must feel.

Again, the key is to form a relationship by doing activities together. You need to see what interests the child and then enter the child's world, as opposed to asking the child to enter your world. While doing activities, you look for ways to value the child. The biological parent and the stepparent should privately have discussions about their approach to parenting, and that should include more than just talking about discipline methods.

If you move into your partner's house you're stepping into a situation that already has its own rules and understandings. You can't be expected to pick up on all of those immediately, so know you will most likely make some mistakes. Everyone needs time to adjust to the situation. Problems may not immediately arise since people tend to be on their best behavior at the very beginning. Over weeks or months, everyone will relax a bit more, and this is where you are likely to experience some clashes.

You may feel apprehensive about being a stepparent, particularly if you have no children of your own. The best way to deal with any child is honestly and at his or her own level. Don't try too hard to suddenly become a terrific parent—that can feel false to the child. Instead, let your relationship grow gradually. Don't worry that you don't know how to be a parent. Not only do you have your partner there to help you, but you have instincts that can help guide you as well. After all, you were once a child, so it isn't that foreign of a condition to you. Kids are just people and want to be treated at face value for who they are.

It's not reasonable for you to expect to love your stepchild immediately. It takes time to have those feelings develop. You're not a bad stepparent if there are things you don't like about your stepchild or that annoy you. You're human, and you should not expect too much of yourself in a difficult situation like this. Try to focus on the positives about your stepchild. Let your relationship just happen. Trying to schedule times to get to know your stepchild can feel artificial. Instead, let things develop organically.

Legal Authority for a Stepparent

A stepparent situation is not only emotionally tricky, but it is legally difficult as well. A long-time stepparent usually develops a close relationship with the child and acts as a third (or second) parent. After the family unit has been together for some time, children often come to see their stepparents as real parents for all intents and purposes. They come to rely on, trust, and love their stepparents in much the same way they do a "real" parent. Because stepfamilies are becoming so common, most people have come to understand and respect the link between stepparent and stepchild.

Despite the closeness of the bond and the growing societal understanding about stepfamilies, the only way an unmarried stepparent can ever have legal authority over a child is to adopt him or her. A stepparent who adopts a child becomes a legal parent in every way. If there is another legal parent in the picture, that parent must consent to the adoption and agree to give up his or her own parental rights. Because of this, stepparent adoptions tend to happen most often in circumstances where the other parent is deceased or has no contact with the child.

Advocacy Tip

There are some states in which stepparents who have been married to the child's legal parent have some legal rights to seek custody or visitation after a divorce. There are no states that make it possible for a stepparent who was not married to the child's parent to seek custody or visitation. In many cases, stepparents develop strong emotional bonds with the children involved, and the breakup of the adult relationship has the consequence of removing an emotional parent from the child's life. It is difficult to legislate emotional bonds, but some recognition of the relationship between child and stepparent would be appropriate. This is something to discuss with your state legislators.

There are some steps that the stepparent's partner can take to offer some legal protection for the stepparent. The parent can execute legal consents that allow the stepparent to make medical decisions for the child and to interact with the school and pick the child up. A parent can also name the stepparent as the guardian in a will. If the other parent has a history of abusing the child, being addicted to drugs, being convicted of crimes, or has had no contact with the child, this may hold up. It's important to note that the court always has final say over guardianship, and if the child's legal parent contests it, the court will have to weigh all the factors and consider who has an existing relationship with the child and who would best be able to care for the child.

Stepsiblings

If you as a single parent find a new partner, there is a good chance that the man or woman you decide to share your life with will also have children. Bringing together your two families can be complicated and wonderful at the same time. It takes a lot of work to mesh two families, but it can be well worth the effort.

When two partners come together and bring children of their own, they create what is called a blended family. Blended families come in all shapes and sizes. The number and ages of the children may vary, and so may their backgrounds and experiences.

Online Stepfamily Support

Online information about stepfamilies can be found at these sites:

- Stepfamily Network *www.stepfamily.net*

- Stepfamily Resource Center *www.stepfamilies.info*

- National Stepfamily Day *www.nationalstepfamilyday.com*

- Stepparent Adoption *www.childwelfare.gov/pubs/f_step.cfm*

- Stepfamily Magazine *www.stepfamilymagazine.com*

When forming a blended family, you need to be able to balance things. When making decisions, you need to consider the feelings and situations of everyone involved and come to a solution that seems to be the best for the most people. It can be challenging to balance so many people's needs and take so many things into consideration in a blended family. Even deciding where to live together as a family can be complicated and confusing. Children are attached to their homes, and the thought of having to move into another child's home can be very threatening and disturbing. If the children need to share a bedroom, this can be even harder to deal with. Everyone in the family has to make an effort to be flexible and understanding—something that can be difficult for a child.

Schedules are a big part of blended families. It's likely that both sets of children have another parent and spend time with that parent. It's also likely that the schedules may not complement each other. It may make sense to adjust visitation schedules so that children will be home together some of the time. In high-conflict families, arranging schedules so that each group of children has time at home alone might also make sense.

There are often problems in blended families with what the children see as equality or fairness. They may feel that the parents treat the other kids differently, hold them to different rules, give them more things, or have lower expectations for them. It's also common to feel as if the other children are loved more or given more attention. Some families deal with these problems head-on by devising family rules that apply to everyone. Other families allow each parent to set rules and expectations for his or her own children.

Stepsiblings may feel as though they are strangers who have somehow been pitted against each other. It can be especially challenging for an only child who suddenly is living in a house with other children and has no idea how to be a sibling or how a sibling should feel. Helping children find common ground and devising a family identity can help ease this to some extent. Conflicts are inevitable though, and it is important to help everyone get through them by emphasizing mutual respect and tolerance.

Stepchildren whose parents were married and then divorced can find the prospect of the new unmarried relationship a bit strange and uncharted. Explaining what your commitment to each other and to the family is can help children understand the permanency of your life together.

Half Siblings

If you and the stepparent decide to have a child together, your children and the new baby will be half siblings. Young children tend not to make many distinctions about how closely related they are to the baby— there's a baby and it is a new brother or sister and that's about all they care about. But the older a child is, the more likely he or she is to think about the "half" effect and acknowledge that while they may share one parent with the new baby, they don't share two parents. The idea of being half of anything can be confusing for a child, so use of this term is not very helpful. Your child has never met someone who was half a mother, or half a grandfather, so the idea of being a half brother or half sister probably doesn't sound too great.

If there is another parent in your child's life, the new baby can present some difficult times. All children have some feelings of being left out when a new baby enters the family, but a baby that equally enthralls the parent and stepparent can leave the child feeling left out or unwanted. The child may feel the stepparent will love the baby more because he or she is related to it and also that the parent is more devoted to the baby because the parents are together. The child can feel that not being related to the stepparent is somehow a strike against the child in the new family situation because it makes him or her different. A child who has time outside the home with the other parent might feel resentful at having to leave when the new baby doesn't have to move from place to place.

Adding a baby is easier to adjust to when the existing children are involved. It is "our" baby—not "my" baby. Children can participate in the process by helping to prepare a room or place for the baby when he or she comes home from the hospital. They might also have some input on the name for the baby—at least veto power to reject names they don't like. Children can also have baby-care tasks that they can help with.

Talking to your child about the new baby and what it means can be helpful. As the parent, you can explain that you love all of your children exactly the same and that will never change. It can also be a good idea for the stepparent to talk to the child about how much he or she loves the child and how the new baby will not change that.

Jealousy, such as vying for Mom and Dad's attention, is a big issue in stepfamilies. Create a routine so that the current children have set times to get parent attention, like reading a story just before bedtime. When the baby arrives, keep these relationship times with the children intact. Also, be watchful about people coming over and fawning over the new baby in the presence of and to the exclusion of the existing children.

Life Lessons

Marni and her daughter Robin had lived alone since Marni and Robin's father, Doug, broke up. Robin saw her father regularly. When Doug moved in with his new partner, Kim, Robin continued to spend time with him on the weekends and slept over at Kim's house. Kim had a daughter a few years younger than Robin, and the two girls did not get along.

Robin often came home and complained to Marni about how she didn't like Kim or Kim's daughter. Sometimes Doug got called into work on days Robin was with him, and when this happened, Robin stayed with Kim. Robin said Kim was always mean to her and ignored her while she played with her own daughter. Robin told Marni that even when Doug was there, he didn't spend time with her. She began to protest about going to Kim's house at all, and one day she locked herself in her room when it was time for her to go.

Marni and Doug had managed to maintain a reasonable parenting relationship, even though they were no longer a couple, so Marni talked to Doug about Robin's feelings. They agreed that some of it was a normal reaction to a new stepparenting situation. Doug agreed he would make more of an effort to be home on days when Robin was there and to spend some time with her alone.

Although Marni wasn't completely comfortable with the idea that Doug had moved on and was living with someone else, Marni's therapist suggested that it might help Robin if Marni and Kim developed some kind of cooperative relationship. Marni was hesitant about this, but invited Kim over for coffee one day while Robin was at school. To her surprise, she found that Kim was a nice person. They talked about how Robin was feeling, and Kim admitted to feeling overwhelmed with suddenly being a stepparent to a child who was not completely embracing her. The women gradually got to know each other and spoke on the phone and had lunch a few times.

Marni and Kim carefully planned some joint family outings. Marni made it a point to always listen to Robin's complaints, but not agree or disagree with her. Eventually, after seeing that her mother had accepted Kim and was able to be pleasant with her, Robin began to come around. It also helped that Kim learned that Robin was really into sewing, and she showed her how to use her state-of-the-art machine. This gave them something to do together and a way to get to know each other. Having a shared interest helped bring them together.

Many years later when Robin graduated from high school, she wrote in the student note section of the program that she was grateful to all three of her parents who had loved and supported her.

Chapter 12
Dealing with Other People

Accepting and loving your life as it is may be something you have achieved, yet dealing with the reactions, comments, and stubbornness of other people may be quite another thing. Although there are certainly many people who have no problems with unmarried families, there are still people who find it hard to understand, or who make your life difficult because of it. It is also true that our culture and society is in many ways designed to recognize and understand two-parent married families, with little room for unmarried families.

Learning to deal with and work around people and entities who make things difficult or cause you to take extra steps to explain yourself can be frustrating. The only way to change things is to live your life the way you believe and continue to stand up for yourself, your family, and your rights.

Schools

Schools work hard to protect the children that they are educating. When your child enters school, there are many forms to fill out. You also need to provide a birth certificate for your child. While schools are accustomed to married parents, stepparents, and divorced parents, there are some schools that are not as accustomed to working with unmarried parents.

The main roadblock you will encounter with schools is their need to know what your custody situation is. If you and your partner live together with your child, this won't be an issue. Schools assume that parents who live together are married. However, if you live separately, the school will ask for details about custody, mainly so that they are clear as to who is allowed to pick up the child from school. If you do not have a custody order, you might consider getting one based on a stipulation (an agreement you present to the court). If you are opposed to doing this, you may both need to sign forms indicating that you both have the same rights with respect to your child.

Medical Personnel

There are a variety of situations in which your nonlegal relationship with your partner can cause confusion while at a hospital or doctor's office. Some advance planning can help you avoid many problems.

Care for Your Child

Rosie O'Donnell tells a story about when her daughter needed stitches and the emergency room personnel would not treat her. Rosie's partner Kelli brought her in and explained she was the parent, but the hospital personnel overheard the child calling Kelli by her first name and noticed she and the child had different last names. Because of this, they would not treat the child, even though Kelli was her legal parent. Because of this incident, Rosie has said on her blog, Kelli changed her last name to O'Donnell.

This kind of situation is not unique. Hospitals will treat children to save their life or limb without parental consent in an emergency situation, but for any other type of care, a parent must give consent. If the hospital is unsure if you are the parent, they will decline to offer treatment.

There are several solutions to this kind of problem. First of all, your pediatrician should be fully informed as to who is a legal parent and who has the parent's permission to obtain treatment. If there is ever a question, you can direct hospital personnel to verify this with your pediatrician. It is also possible to carry a copy of a birth certificate or adoption papers with you at all times—such as in the child's diaper bag or in your glove compartment. If you are not the legal parent of your child, you need to make sure you have a copy of the permission to seek medical treatment authorization with you just in case.

Care for You or Your Partner

Another problem that can arise with medical personnel is your access to your partner. If one of you enters the hospital, visits may be restricted to close family, and if you aren't married, you won't qualify. It can be a good idea to ask your primary care doctor to note in the file that your partner is your next of kin. When entering a hospital, always be sure to name your partner as your next of kin on hospital forms.

Having an advance directive (also sometimes called a health care proxy, living will, or health care power of attorney) that names your partner as the person who can make your health care decisions is another important step you can take to protect yourselves. If you do not have a form that meets your state requirements, the hospital will turn to your partner's legal next of kin, such as parents, to make important decisions, such as whether to continue life support. If you do not have an advance directive, you can pay an attorney to complete one, or you can find information online at *www.USLivingWillRegistry.com*. An advance directive names the person you select to make decisions for you if you are not able, and it also usually specifies what your wishes are in particular situations so that there can be no confusion over your specific wishes. You and your partner should each have one. Once you have one completed, it is important to keep it in a safe place that is easily accessible. You can give a copy to your doctor to keep on file, and you can also use the U.S. Living Will Registry to keep it online and accessible to any medical personnel.

It is a good idea to sign a form at your doctor's office giving your partner access to all of your medical records so that your partner can talk to your health care provider for you if it is ever necessary. Under HIPAA (the health care privacy act) no one can have access to your records without your permission, so you have to sign a form in advance.

Health Insurance

With the high cost of medical expenses, health insurance is an extremely important issue for many families.

Health Insurance for Partners

A disadvantage of not being married is not being able to be carried on each other's health insurance policies. It's likely that one of you will have a family policy that also covers your child. Adding a married partner to that policy would have zero cost; however, because you are not married, you can't add your partner. He or she has to have a separate policy. This can be very expensive, particularly as health insurance premiums continue to rise and employers pay less and less of the costs. If you are a gay couple, you may be able to obtain coverage if your company has a policy or if your state has a law requiring coverage for domestic partners. However, most domestic partner provisions cover only same-sex couples and do not apply to heterosexual unmarried partners.

Advocacy Tip

Public awareness of the inability of same-sex couples to share health insurance has made a big public splash, and as a result more and more companies, municipalities, and states are making health insurance available to same-sex domestic partners. Despite this, the same benefits are not being extended to heterosexual partners, even when it is extended to same-sex couples. The rationale often is that you should marry to get these benefits, but denying benefits to unmarried couples is a huge public health crisis. There are over 3 million unmarried coupled people without health insurance. Offering benefits to same-sex couples but not to heterosexual couples is discriminatory.

If you are in this situation, talk about it. Let your employer, coworkers, state legislators, city legislators, and neighbors know of the discrimination you face and how it affects your health and your financial situation. Only if people talk about it will awareness be increased and changes made.

The unavailability of health insurance can be a particular problem if one of you is a stay-at-home parent with no employer. All states now offer state-sponsored health insurance programs for children, and many offer these same programs to uninsured adults as well. These programs are low cost or no cost and are income based. For more information, see *www.insurekidsnow.gov*. Buying an insurance policy directly from an insurance company is insanely expensive, so if there is a way for you to get a group rate, such as through the local chamber of commerce or through a professional organization you belong to, strongly consider it. If this isn't an option, you might consider a high-deductible policy that will cover you for major health disasters.

If you are able to receive domestic partner health insurance, it is considered taxable income, so you'll need to report it as such on your income tax forms.

If you and your partner want to be able to make calls, deal with claims, or ask for referrals for each other from your health insurance company, ask them for a form you can sign and keep on file to authorize this.

Medicaid Planning

Although you might be young and do not feel a need to worry about Medicaid for many years, it is an important issue for unmarried families. Currently, Medicaid laws require people to use up their assets first before qualifying for Medicaid coverage. Part of this involves the home; however, Medicaid law has an exception that allows a spouse to remain in the home even if the other spouse is on Medicaid. Unmarried couples are not eligible for this exception. It is a good idea to talk with an attorney who specializes in Medicaid planning. He or she can help you and your partner organize your assets and make plans to protect yourselves should Medicaid ever be an issue.

Health Insurance for Your Child

If your child is carried on your partner's health insurance policy, be certain that the company has a written form from your partner stating you are the child's other parent and have complete access to all records and information. It is also a good idea to request an additional ID card for your child to carry with you so that should you need to seek medical care for your child when your partner is not available, you will have the current insurance information with you.

Businesses and Business Entities

Because the notion of an unmarried, committed couple is incomprehensible to some people, you may encounter some businesses (or the people that work for them) that have a hard time understanding your situation. Although it's easy to get annoyed with people who can't wrap their minds around your situation, there is usually a solution if you are patient and work through the options.

Banks and Investments

Anyone can open a joint account with anyone else. You and your partner can have joint accounts and you and your child can have joint accounts (if you do open accounts for your child, be sure to do so under the United Gift to Minors Act or the United Transfers to Minors Act since these ensure the money is controlled by an adult and offer tax protections). If you prefer to have separate accounts, you can complete a power-of-attorney form at the bank that will allow your partner access to your individual account—this can be very helpful for times when you can't get to the bank or during illness. It's also possible to simply exchange passwords for your online banking access so you can handle each other's account electronically.

If you and your partner share a residence, it may make sense to share at least one bank account for household expenses. How you contribute to that account is up to you. Some couples equally contribute. Other couples rely on one partner to contribute more since he or she earns more. Some couples like to maintain a joint savings account as well. If you live apart and share parenting expenses, you may wish to have a joint account for that. As with bank accounts, you and your partner can have joint investment accounts.

When setting up joint accounts, you may wish to be sure you set them up as joint with right of survivorship, so if one partner dies, the ownership of the account passes directly to the other partner.

You may not be able to designate each other as beneficiaries for your pension plans. Be sure to check with the plan administrator to determine if this is possible or not. If not, you can always designate your child, and the other parent would be his or her financial guardian anyhow.

Creditors

You and your partner can open joint credit card accounts if you apply together. You can also request a card to be issued to your partner on your account (this can be very convenient if one of you has bad credit and encounters difficulty getting credit cards). While it is convenient to have some joint credit, it may not make sense to have all your credit be joint. If you open a joint account, you are both liable for the account, and any problems with it will appear on both of your credit reports. Since you are not legally married, individual accounts will not affect the other partner's credit rating.

Utilities

If you desire, it is usually easy to get utility bills to be issued in both of your names. Utilities commonly do this for roommates, which is how they should view your situation. Having utilities in both names allows either of you to contact them to dispute a bill, arrange for service, or make changes to the account.

Car Rentals

When married people rent a car, they can list the other spouse as an additional driver at no extra charge. In order for your partner to be able to drive a car you rent, you must list him or her as an additional driver (or any accidents occurring while he or she drives will not be covered) at added expense. Many car rental companies charge an extra fee to add a person to the rental who is not your spouse. What many people do not realize is that many car rental companies will add a domestic partner on for free if you both live at the same address. When you rent the car, explain you are domestic partners and show proof that you have the same address, and you may be able to list the second partner at no cost. Some companies will only provide this benefit if you both are AAA members. It never hurts to ask about adding a domestic partner. It is not a good idea to lie and say you are married because if there is an accident and it is revealed you lied, you could be liable.

Taxes

Because you and your partner are not married, you cannot file joint tax returns, even though you may be sharing the same home and raising your child together. You will need to decide who claims your child as an exemption. You can alternate this every year if you wish, but only one of you can claim your child each year.

If you share expenses, such as a mortgage or home equity loan, you should try to keep clear records that show your individual contribution to those deductions so that if you are audited you can prove you paid a portion of it.

Power of Attorney

It is a good idea for you and your partner to complete power-of-attorney forms, which will allow you to handle each other's business and financial matters. There are several types of powers of attorney. A springing power of attorney only becomes valid upon the happening of an event—such as an illness or inability to transact business. You could choose a general power of attorney, which becomes effective immediately and will allow you to handle each other's affairs at any time.

Friends

How your friends react to your relationship can color some of your feelings about it as well. Friends should be there to support you and love you as you go through your life, but if you have a friend who is not supportive, you may need to consider how healthy that friendship is.

The reactions of your friends may be tied to the types of choices people in your social group make. If you are in your twenties and living in New York City, you can expect your friends to have a different understanding and familiarity with unmarried couples than if you live in a farming community in Nebraska. While these types of demographics can impact the reaction, it is interesting to note that there is a rise of unmarried couples just where you might not expect to see it—among couples in their sixties and seventies. It's not uncommon for people in this age group to choose to remain an unmarried couple so as not to affect Social Security or pension payments from a deceased spouse.

Whether your friends view your relationship as normal or out of the norm, the only ones who can make it work are you and your partner.

When your child makes friends and you arrange play dates or get-togethers, you will get to know the parents of the friend. It's hard to know what to expect from these parents—they may be welcoming and friendly, or they may be suspicious and difficult. The best way to approach an unknown situation is with a positive attitude. If you are comfortable and happy with your life, you can convey that attitude to others—and to your child, who will be in this situation with you.

Introductions

When you and your partner were together before you had a child, you might have introduced each other to other people as "my boyfriend" or "my girlfriend." Once you became committed to each other, you might have changed that designation to "my partner." When they have a child together, some people feel uncomfortable introducing the other partner as a boyfriend or girlfriend, because those words don't seem to show how serious the relationship is. On the other hand, some heterosexual couples are hesitant to use the word "partner," since they feel it is most often used by gay couples. One option some people use is to introduce the other person as "my daughter's father" or "my son's mother." However, this description makes it sound as if your only relationship to each other is through your child, and it may give the impression you are not a couple.

Some committed couples take to referring to each other as their "spouse," "husband," or "wife," even though they are not married, simply because it is more comprehensible to the people they are talking to. It's certainly shorter than introducing someone as "Joe, my live-in boyfriend with whom I have a son." If you are opposed to the idea of marriage though, using marriage terminology might not appeal to you. Some people use the term "my fiancé(e)," which conveys the level of commitment involved, while making it understood that you are not married. The problem with this terminology, of course, is you will get a lot of people asking you, "When's the wedding?" Sometimes couples use the term "my common-law spouse," even if they may not have actually met the common-law marriage requirements, or do not live in a state in which common-law marriage is recognized (see Chapter 13 for more information on common-law marriage). Some couples introduce each other as "my lady" or "my man" or "the love of my life," which conveys the commitment level of the relationship.

If you and your partner live in separate homes but are committed to each other, you may find it even more difficult to concisely explain this relationship in terms people are familiar with. You may not need to; ask yourself if other people really need to know the details of how you've worked out your relationship and living arrangement. If you feel it is important, referring to the other person as a boyfriend, girlfriend, or fiancé(e) is an adequate description that fits with the idea of living separately.

Ultimately, how you choose to refer to each other is something that will evolve out of your own experiences and your own comfort level in various situations. You might want to discuss this with your partner, since you might feel uncomfortable with some descriptors. What is most important is that you use words you are comfortable with.

Extended Family

When you partner with someone, his or her family becomes your family in many ways. You will probably spend many holidays with each other's families. Once you are parents, you will find that your lives are even more connected.

Some families may be hesitant to completely accept you or your partner since in their eyes, you have not made a final commitment to each other because you are not married. Some families have rules about holiday gift exchanges that might exclude you or your partner. Often large families have a rule or tradition that only those people who have married into the family can participate in the gift exchange. This rule can become awkward if you and your partner are there year after year without wedding rings yet are life partners raising children together. Your children may eventually be curious as to why one parent is excluded. If this type of situation bothers you, bring it up with your family. Express your concerns and how the family tradition affects you and makes you feel and ask to participate if it is important to you.

At weddings, you or your partner may be encouraged to go up to attempt to catch the bouquet or garter since you are both technically unmarried. If you feel comfortable doing this, by all means, do so. If you don't want to participate, simply saying "No thanks, I'm taken" usually solves it.

Older relatives may have a hard time understanding your relationship and may try to convince you that you need to get married. Some people react with a nod and smile, while others take it as an opportunity to explain the situation. Choose the solution that makes you most comfortable, while taking into account the limited experience and good intentions of the person you're talking to (half-deaf, frail, ninety-five-year-old Aunt Sally may not be the person to prove your point with).

Because you and your partner are not married, you may not be sure how to refer to your partner's family. Your partner's mother is for all intents and purposes your mother-in-law, and if those words work for you, go with them. It's possible that you or she might not be comfortable with that terminology. If you've been encouraged to do so, you might call your partner's parents Mom and Dad or you might call them by their first names. How you introduce them to other people might be tricky. If you introduce them to someone who knows you and your partner, you can simply say, "These are Mark's parents, Sharon and Joe." If you introduce them to someone who does not know you and your partner, you could introduce them as your partner's parents, your in-laws, or your fiancé(e)'s parents.

While finding the right words can sometimes be a challenge, what is more important is what your relationship is like with your partner's family. Some parents are never able to accept their child's partner as a true member of the family (and this is also true of married couples as well, so it's not just something necessarily caused by your unmarried status). If your partner's parents or your parents have difficulty accepting your relationship, you can tell them how you feel, ask for their love and acceptance, and then move on with your life.

Many parents feel more attached to their children's partners when grandchildren enter the picture. Being a link to the next generation can solidify a partner's role in the family structure. When older generations begin to see you as a true family unit with children, they may be more accepting of your situation.

👫 Life Lessons

Brandon and Marielle were parents of a nine-year-old girl. They considered themselves to be best friends, partners, and parents who lived separate lives. After several different arrangements, they both lived in the same duplex building, in separate apartments. Brandon owned the duplex, and Marielle was technically his tenant, although she did not pay rent. Instead, their arrangement was that the apartment was Brandon's major financial contribution.

One day, Brandon was in a car accident. He had Marielle's contact information listed in his cell phone under ICE (in case of emergency, a designation emergency responders urge people to enter into their phones). Marielle got to the hospital and was not permitted to see him because she was not his spouse or relative. She was shocked and frightened because who would make decisions for him? Then she remembered that years ago when they had their wills written, their attorney had prepared advance directives. Marielle went home and found the document in Brandon's safe and returned to the hospital with it. The document gave her authority to visit him in the hospital and make all decisions for him.

Brandon recovered from his accident with Marielle by his side. When their attorney prepared the advance directive, he also had them prepare powers of attorney. Because she had this form, Marielle was able to cash Brandon's checks and pay his bills while he was in the hospital. Their lives were terribly disrupted because of the accident, but because they had prepared these documents, Marielle was able to handle Brandon's health care and financial matters so that he could focus on getting well.

Chapter 13
Planning for the Future

The wonderful thing about being parents is that it links you to the future in a very invested and real way. Planning for your own future, as well as that of your children can seem a bit daunting sometimes, but it is always important.

Inheritance

Each state has intestacy laws, which dictate how a person's estate is divided if they die without a will. These laws generally split the estate among spouse and children. You and your partner will have no right to inherit from each other without a will because partners are not recognized as spouses for the purposes of the laws. Your child has the right to inherit from legal parents under these laws. If one of you is not a legal parent, you can make a provision for your child in your will, which will ensure that he or she is your heir. It is also possible to set up trusts for children or partners to ensure that they are taken care of.

Benefits

There are a variety of benefits that married couples are entitled to, such as pensions and Social Security. There is no way to affect these benefits for unmarried couples. Children are also entitled to these benefits, but in order to receive them, a child must be the legal child of the parent the benefit stems from. Legal children are also entitled to collect under malpractice, wrongful death, or personal injury suits settled after a parent's death, but unmarried partners would have no stake in these suits.

Guardianship and Wills

Chapter 10 discusses wills and guardianship as important for solo parents, but this is also an important issue for families in which there are two parents.

A will is important for you and your partner because it allows you to leave property to each other. You can pass almost all kinds of property through your will (with things like life insurance benefits and trusts being handled separately). You can also use your will to leave property to your child or children in any amount you would like, whether they are your legal children or not. If you and your partner are leaving your estates to each other, you should talk with your attorney about inserting a provision in your wills regarding simultaneous death. It's not pleasant to think about, but there is always the chance that the two of you could lose your lives in a car accident together. A simultaneous death provision lays out, for purposes of probating the wills, who legally died first, and affects where your property may eventually end up.

For parents, wills also offer the opportunity to designate a guardian who will be responsible for your child should something happen to you. If you and your partner are both legal parents, you don't need to name each other as guardians of first choice, but if you feel there will be some kind of question about this by family members, you can do so. If one of you is not a legal parent, it is absolutely essential that the legal parent name the nonlegal parent as guardian, because otherwise that parent has no real assurances of being named guardian.

When you choose a guardian, it is important that you talk to the person and make sure it is something he or she would feel comfortable doing. In addition to naming a guardian, you should choose an alternate guardian in case the person you choose is unable to take on that responsibility.

Adding Siblings to Your Family

Families with one child are in the minority, but it is a situation that works very well for some. Not all families are able to afford the extra time and expense involved in having more than one child. But if you and your partner have the means and decide to add more children to your family, you are sure to experience more joy.

There are a variety of ways to add children to your family—birth, adoption, half siblings, and stepsiblings. However you expand your family, you can expect to need to make some adjustments. The first consideration may be your living arrangements. If you and your partner live apart, you may need to have some help in the beginning—whether this is from your partner or other family and friends.

Another important consideration is financial. Although a baby does not add huge expenses immediately, in the long term, the impact is significant. When you think about adding a child to your family, it may be helpful to construct a budget to help you see what your increased costs will be and how you will manage them. You and your partner may need to renegotiate how you share household and children's costs.

The legal relationship of your children to each other is something else to consider. When you give birth to or adopt a child, he or she becomes a legal sibling of your existing child, but a stepsibling is not considered legally related to his or her stepsiblings.

Marriage

Statistics from the U.S. Census Bureau show that 70 percent of couples who live together for five or more years eventually do marry. For some people, marriage is a step in a continuum, while for others it is something they do not want. Some couples live together and eventually decide they do want to marry. For other couples, marriage is never something that is part of the plan. It's a good idea for you and your partner to fully understand each other's feelings about marriage so that there won't be any misunderstandings along the way.

Interestingly, statistics show that women who are employed are more likely to have their cohabitation turn into marriage. Couples who live together and then marry have a higher rate of divorce (24 percent) than couples who marry without living together (18 percent), but these numbers only hold true for first marriages. There is no change in the divorce rate for couples who cohabit before a second marriage.

There are many benefits to a legal marriage, many of which have been pointed out throughout this book. What is difficult for some people to quantify, though, is that there are benefits to an unmarried partnership as well, and whether you choose to marry is a personal choice. There is no question that getting legally married offers benefits, and each couple must weigh those benefits against what they personally see as the benefits of remaining unmarried.

Should you and your partner decide to marry, you automatically qualify for the many benefits given to married couples under state and federal law. Marrying does not change the legal parentage of your children, however. Should your marriage end, all property is considered marital property as of the date of your marriage, not the date your cohabitation began.

Marriage Legal Benefits

There are over a thousand state and federal benefits given to married couples, which unmarried couples do not have access to. These include:

- Ability to file joint state and federal tax returns and to create a family partnership for the purpose of tax laws

- Accidental death benefit for the surviving spouse of a government employee

- Bereavement leave when your spouse dies

- Consent to postmortem examination

- Continuation of rights under existing homestead leases

- Criminal injuries compensation

- Death benefit for surviving spouse for government employee

- Exemption from conveyance tax

- Family leave to care for an ill spouse

- Family rates on insurance

- Health insurance benefits through your spouse

- Hospital visitation of your spouse

- Immigration rights

- Making, revoking, and objecting to anatomical gifts

- Marital deduction on estate tax

- Marital trusts for estate tax purposes

- Payment of worker's compensation benefits after death

- Permission to make arrangements for burial or cremation

- Right of election against the spouse's estate

- Right to inherit property

- Right to own real property as tenants of entirety (where each owns the entire thing)

■ Right to sue for tort and death by wrongful act

■ Spousal privilege and confidential marriage communications

■ Spousal immigration benefits

■ Veterans' benefits for spouses

■ Visiting rights in jails

Common-Law Marriage

Common-law marriage is often misunderstood. Many people think that if you and your partner live together for a certain number of years (often seven or ten), you magically become legally married in the eyes of the law. Most states do not recognize common-law marriage, and those that do have stricter requirements than simply living together.

Common-Law Marriage States

Common-law marriages exist only in the following states:

■ Alabama

■ Colorado

■ District of Columbia

■ Georgia

■ Idaho

■ Iowa

■ Kansas

■ Montana

■ New Hampshire

■ Ohio

■ Oklahoma

■ Pennsylvania

■ Rhode Island

- South Carolina

- Texas

- Utah

States that recognize common-law marriage usually have three requirements to meet in order to be considered married. You must live together as husband and wife for a specified period of time (in some states you must also actually agree to be married), you must hold yourselves out as married (by introducing each other as "my husband" or "my wife"), and you must have documents that reflect the fact that you have held yourselves out as spouses—such as leases, insurance policies, tax returns, and so on, which specifically refer to you as married. If you meet these requirements, you can be considered legally married if you live in a state that recognizes common-law marriages. You can then access all the benefits legally married couples have. If you break up, you can just separate, or you can go through a divorce procedure.

If you're opposed to marriage of any sort, you don't automatically become common-law married partners if you meet the requirements. It only comes into play if you want it to—if you seek to be legally recognized as a married couple (no one goes around asking if you meet the requirements and then stamping "married" on your forehead). Generally you're only legally considered to have a common-law marriage if a court recognizes it as such. You can certainly assume you have a common-law marriage and act as if it is legal, but you're not absolutely guaranteed that legal status unless a court gives it. Until that point, it can always be challenged.

There are some situations when common-law marriage could work against you. If you and your partner meet the requirements and one of you is sued, the other person's assets could be taken if it is proved that you have met common-law marriage requirements. Also, if you break up, your partner could take you to court for divorce, even if you never really considered yourselves to be common-law married. Your partner could claim part of your estate, even if you leave him or her nothing in your will, under the state spousal right of election law, which gives a spouse an absolute right to a percent of the estate regardless of whether he or she is written out of the will.

If you live together in a common-law state and do not want to be common-law married, you can sign an agreement with your spouse that clearly says you are aware of the common-law marriage law and you specifically do not wish to be in a common-law marriage together and neither of you intends to be married. It is a good idea to get such a document notarized and then store it in a safe place.

If you are recognized in your home state as having a common-law marriage and have sought out that designation, it is likely you will be recognized by other states as being married as well. Do some research to understand what your specific state requirements for common-law marriage are, or talk to an attorney who can discuss them with you. The laws in some states apply only to common-law marriages formed before or after a certain date, so be certain to learn about such restrictions.

Domestic Partnerships

Domestic partnerships are increasingly becoming available to gay couples, but the trend is not continuing as strongly for heterosexual couples, and it is rare for domestic partnership laws to apply to heterosexual couples. States and municipalities create domestic partnership laws that allow couples to register their partnership and receive certain rights and benefits, such as hospital visitation rights, access to health care benefits from the partner, and inheritance rights. The rights granted vary by state and municipality, so if you qualify, check the law to find out what rights it gives you.

States with Heterosexual Domestic Partnerships

- California (only for those over age sixty-two)

- New Jersey (only for those over age sixty-two)

- Oregon

- Washington (only for those over age sixty-two)

- Washington, D.C.

    In addition, New York State has a law that allows heterosexual domestic partners hospital visitation rights.

    Many municipalities offer domestic partnerships, so check with yours to find out if it includes heterosexual couples.

If domestic partnership is available to you, you may consider it in order to receive the benefits and rights it confers. If you are against government involvement in your private life, it might not be something you are interested in at all. Obtaining a domestic partnership has no impact on your children or your relationship with your children.

Advocacy Tip

Many people are unaware of the fact that heterosexual couples cannot obtain a domestic partnership and don't understand why it would be beneficial. You can raise awareness of this issue by talking to people about it and writing to your legislators. If your city or state has a domestic partnership law in place, talk about how these benefits are denied to heterosexual couples and how having the benefits would be helpful.

It's also important to note that when you live with a partner, whether you register your relationship with the state or city or not, you create your own domestic partnership. You and your partner can create your own agreement or contract with each other to develop guidelines for how you will live together, share expenses, and share responsibilities.

Polyfamilies

If you or your partner is considering entering into a polyamorous relationship or polyfidelity (or if you are already in one), you may wonder how this is handled in terms of legal rights. Polygamy is illegal in all states; however, there are no laws against living with more than one partner. It is not possible to be legally married to more than one person, but it is possible to live with and love more than one person. Polyamory and polyfidelity are less socially acceptable than having an unmarried partner, but many people still do find happiness in this way.

Polyfamilies can take the same steps to protect themselves as other unmarried families—wills, advance directives, powers of attorney, permission to seek medical treatment for a child, and more. The only difference might be that you authorize more than one person to seek medical care for your child, make decisions for you, or handle your affairs. One thing to remember when naming more than one person in these types of situations is that you create the possibility of them not being able to agree about what to do. When possible, naming just one person is simpler, and you could then name the other person (or people) as an alternate.

When a child is born into a polyfamily, he or she has legal parents and nonlegal parents. Some polyfamilies with more than one adult male may not know who is the father of a child, and in that case, either you can leave the name of the father blank on the birth certificate or you can have a paternity test to determine it and have it legally entered. No matter who is the father, all the men in the family can act as parents. Just as with traditional stepparents though, stepparents in polyfamilies have limited legal rights with respect to the child.

Some parents worry that raising a child in a polyfamily could be construed as neglectful or abusive, since polyfamilies do not fall into generally acceptable mores. As with any consenting adult couple, what the adults in the family do in the privacy of their bedrooms has no effect on their fitness to parent. Parents have the freedom to raise their children in a polyfamily if they wish. Should you encounter a custody battle with the child's other parent who is not in the polyfamily, though, you are likely to face a lot of opposition and misunderstanding.

👫 Life Lessons

Dalia and Duval were dating when Dalia became pregnant with their daughter. They decided to live together and moved in about halfway through the pregnancy. As they got older and their daughter grew, they settled into their life together. They thought of themselves as married, even though they never had a wedding. They naturally began referring to each other as wife and husband and instead of explaining they weren't married, simply let people think they were.

One day, Dalia's sister read an article in a national newspaper about common-law marriages and showed it to Dalia. None of them had ever really considered common-law marriage as being applicable or important, but the article talked about all the rights and benefits married people have, which unmarried people do not have. Dalia wondered if she and Duval were common-law married. She looked it up on the Internet and learned her state did not have common-law marriages.

She and Duval began to talk about marriage. After reading the article, Dalia was worried about all the things they were missing out on. If Duval died in a construction accident at work, she would have no right to benefits or to file a lawsuit if his death was caused by negligence. If something happened to him, she wouldn't be able to collect Social Security. She was shocked to learn that if he died, she would have to pay taxes on the house if she inherited his part of it. Finally she and Duval decided that they should just get married to make it legal. They had a simple ceremony and a small party just for family and friends afterward. They both still felt a little ambivalent about marriage, but agreed that it made sense to take advantage of the protections it could offer them and their family.

Chapter 14
Ending Your Unmarried Relationship

Should you reach a point where your relationship is ending, it is likely you will have a lot of concerns and questions about finances, custody, and ways to help you and your child cope. The end of a relationship is a difficult time for everyone involved, and coping with the emotional trauma is a long-term process. Getting a grip on some of the day-to-day and financial issues can help you take control of your life.

Parenting while Having Relationship Problems

Many relationships go through difficult times. Every relationship has its ups and downs. People go through periods when they do not feel as close to each other or when they feel dissatisfied with their lives. Just because you experience a difficult time does not mean you are heading for a breakup or the end of your relationship. Relationship problems often can be fixed or moved past.

When you and your partner experience difficult times, it is very likely your child will, on some level, be aware of it. The relationship of the adults in the home has a deep and profound impact on the children in that home. The best thing you can do is try to minimize the impact of your problems on your child. This means you should try not to fight in front of your child and you should never speak derogatorily about the other parent to your child. Your child is not a sounding board or a friend—he or she is not there to listen to your troubles, to take your side, or to cheer you up. Adult relationship problems should be handled by the adults.

That being said, you are first a person and second a parent. Sometimes you are going to have an argument in front of your child or you are going to get very annoyed at the other parent and your child will be made aware of it. If this happens, don't beat yourself up. You're human and human beings sometimes have feelings that are hard to manage. It is okay to make mistakes—forgive yourself and move forward with good intentions.

Despite your best intentions, there are times when your child will sense there is something wrong and will ask questions about it. It is okay to explain that parents are people too, who sometimes get upset with each other. Stress that it has nothing to do with your child and is not his or her fault. Do not talk to your child about a breakup unless it is actually happening. Never ask your child his or her opinion about a potential breakup, or try to convince your child that the other parent is behind the problems.

Deciding to Break Up

Deciding to end your relationship is a painful decision. If you aren't sure whether to end it or not, couples counseling can be very helpful, as can individual counseling. Take your time to make this decision—it isn't something to rush into.

One thing people always wonder about when they are contemplating ending their relationship is what kind of impact it will have on the child. In recent years there have been studies that seem to indicate that divorce is detrimental to children. Everyone agrees that divorce or separation is not the ideal situation for any family. Studies are great, but each person needs to make the decision that is right for him or her, and his or her family. Living in a high-conflict family where there is domestic violence, verbal abuse, lack of respect, or emotional harm is very detrimental to a child. It is also healthier for a child to have two parents who are happy and confident and live in separate homes than to have two miserable parents under one roof. When deciding whether to end your relationship, you should take into account how it will affect your child, but you also do need to make a decision that is based on what is best for everyone involved. Happy parents raise happy kids.

Resolving Custody and Visitation

When you and your partner separate, you will need to create a parenting plan that will spell out how you will each spend time with your child. It is very easy to let this decision develop into a symbol of the way you feel about each other, instead of making a plan that works best for your child. If the parenting plan is well designed, no one wins or loses. It is not a contest to decide who is the better parent, or who treated the other parent the worst. It is a way to organize your time so that your child can spend time with both parents.

If you and the other parent are able to create this plan yourselves, it will be better for everyone. You understand your child and have an intimate understanding of your schedules. Any plan you create is going to be much more customized than one created by a judge or lawyer. If you and your partner can step up and take control of this situation, it will be better for everyone. Chapter 9 offers important tips and information about how to create a parenting plan.

When you break up, it is easy to look for ways to hurt each other, and it can be very tempting to use your child as a tool to do so. Doing this is very detrimental to your child and to your own relationship with your child. You need to try to think separately about your relationship with your ex and your child's relationship with your ex. They are two separate things and need to be handled and treated completely differently.

Child and Spousal Support

When you and your partner separate, you can make decisions on your own about child and spousal support. Going to court is an alternative, not a requirement. In fact, if neither of you want there to be any kind of spousal or child support, nothing says you have to set anything up. It is a right, not an obligation.

Each state has child support laws that spell out what percentage of income a noncustodial parent should pay in child support. Looking at these guidelines may be helpful for you and your ex. You could use the guidelines to give you an idea of what child support is normally like and then choose to follow it, or create your plan.

If you create a child support plan on your own outside of the court system, you need to be aware of several things. First of all, if there is no court order, the plan is not enforceable at all. You can't do anything if the other parent doesn't pay. Secondly, payments you receive as child support that are not directed by a court order could cause tax ramifications for you. Child support paid pursuant to a court order is not deductible by the person paying it or reportable as income by the person receiving it, but payments outside a court order could be construed as income. There are various ways around this for people who wish to get around it. Payments made in cash are not very traceable and payments made on behalf of a child, such as to a school, daycare, or doctor's office are not likely to be traceable either.

In addition to child support, some unmarried couples who break up agree on spousal support payments. There is no court mechanism for spousal support if you are unmarried (unless you try palimony, see later in this chapter, or are able to prove a common-law marriage, see Chapter 13), but that doesn't mean you can't agree that some kind of spousal support is needed. Again, as with informal child support, the person receiving the money could face tax ramifications. And again, these types of payments are not enforceable in court. There are a variety of ways spousal support can be arranged—cash payments, paying tuition for an ex, paying bills for an ex, and so on.

Dividing Assets and Debts

If you and your ex had joint assets or debts, you will need to find a way to divide them. This can be difficult and drawn out if you let it.

Considering Tax Ramifications

Because you are not married, there can be tax ramifications related to the way you divide up property and debts from your relationship. For example, if you have a joint bank account and decide that as part of your property agreement the entire thing will go to Partner A, Partner A could be hit with a tax bill or gift tax problems. The contributions Partner B made to the account are transferred to Partner A, who is not a spouse. This is technically income to Partner A. You face the same problem with debts. If Partner A becomes solely responsible for the balance on the Visa bill and Partner B was responsible for some of those charges, the payment of that bill is a monetary benefit to Partner B. Note that you can give up to $12,000 to any one person each year without invoking gift tax (this is based on 2007 rates—the rates change each year, so Google them for the current year).

The Meaning of Belongings

Deciding how to divide assets and belongings can be difficult. Very often people in a breakup become consumed with this. Belongings become symbolic, and people fight over them in irrational ways. It is very important to take a deep breath once in a while and remind yourself it is all just stuff. You can always get more stuff at some point. Whether you end up with the wide-screen TV in no way comments on what kind of person you are and whether or not you were the one at fault in the breakup. Certainly there are some things that have sentimental value, but it is too easy to fool yourself into thinking you are emotionally attached to each and every thing in your house. Try to separate out what you want and what you need.

How to Divide Property

The best way to divide property is to take a hard look at who can really use it. If you're moving to a condo, you will have no use for the lawn mower. If your partner is moving south, he or she doesn't need the snow blower. Children's belongings should, for the most part, stay at the house where the children will spend most of their time. It may make sense to keep sets together—splitting up the china set decreases the value of it.

It can be useful to make up a list of the items you have not been able to agree on and then have a meeting to try to divide them up. Try to divide things so that when you total the value of all belongings, cash, and accounts, you end up with bottom-line numbers that are fairly equal for each person.

Debts

Dividing up debts is even less fun than dividing up belongings because, after all, who wants to take on debt? There are several ways to think about your joint debts. You can divide them so that the person who benefits from the item being paid for takes on the debt—so that the person who gets the car takes the car payment, and the person who stays in the house takes the mortgage. You can also try to divide them in an equal manner. If you have debts you consider joint but that are in separate names, you can transfer those or pay them off for the other person (see discussion earlier in this chapter about tax ramifications). Note that paying a debt for another person is technically considered income for the person it benefits; however, the IRS has made it clear that paying tuition or medical bills for another person is specifically not considered income to the person benefiting.

Mediation

If you and your partner are having trouble agreeing about the many decisions you are facing as part of your separation, consider mediation. Because family court is only available to you for some of the issues you are facing (see later in this chapter), it is difficult to resolve everything there. Court is also a confrontational win/lose situation. Mediation is a cooperative process in which no one loses and both parties come to a resolution together that works best for them and their families.

When you mediate, you and your partner sit down and talk with a mediator, who is usually a therapist or attorney who has training and experience in mediation. The mediator is not there to make judgments or decisions. Instead, he or she is there to help you work toward a solution yourselves. The goal is empowerment.

Mediation is an affordable alternative, particularly when you compare it to a trial. Because mediation emphasizes working together and finding a solution you can both agree on, you leave mediation with respect for each other. You are not encouraged to tear each other apart, hurt each other, or air your very private grievances in public. Instead, you are encouraged to look for solutions.

Family mediators are trained to work with all kinds of families—married, divorced, gay, unmarried, stepfamilies, and so on. Mediation gives you the freedom to make choices on your own, without having to fit into some preconceived framework.

Parents who mediate find that they are able to better work together as parents afterward. Mediation is also important because not only does it help you resolve whatever your current disagreement is, but it teaches you dispute-resolution skills. If you encounter problems in the future with your parenting plan, you will know how to sit down and work through those problems. Couples who go to court do not learn those skills and instead are encouraged to run back to court every time they butt heads. Doing so is not healthy for you or your child.

Mediation is empowering. It allows you and your partner, who have created this family and this life together, to decide how you will now alter it together. No one tells you what to do—you decide on your own. This can be very freeing.

Mediation helps you provide a positive example to your child of how people should approach and work through problems. You don't run away from problems, expect other people to solve them, let them overwhelm you, or allow them to send you over the edge. Instead, you face them and you look for solutions and compromises. You treat the other person with respect and honor.

Mediation is not for every couple. Couples who have experienced domestic violence are not appropriate for mediation because there is no way to be sure one partner is not being intimidated. Couples where one partner is not able to speak up for him- or herself may also not be appropriate candidates for mediation because the process requires each person to say what they need and what will work for them.

Court Alternatives

If you and your partner are not able to work through your problems on your own or through mediation, you are left with court as your only option. This isn't the optimal solution, but for some couples, nothing else works.

Custody and Visitation

Custody and visitation cases are heard in family court. Any couple who are the legal parents of a child can come to family court. It is for unmarried as well as married families. Many people who go to family court do so without an attorney, so the court personnel is used to working with people who represent themselves. They will help you fill out the necessary forms.

When you appear in family court, it is likely that the court will issue a temporary order of custody and visitation. Usually this order seeks to maintain the status quo—wherever the child is living, the court wants to keep him or her there while the case is pending. If there is a problem with the status quo, you need to speak up and let the judge know the problem.

The court will then eventually schedule you for a settlement meeting, and in some states you will be sent to mandatory mediation. This is because the majority of cases settle before a trial, so the court wants to encourage the settlement process. If you cannot reach an agreement, your case will eventually be slated for a trial. A law guardian, or guardian ad litem, will be appointed to represent your child's interests in the case. You will each have to present evidence and testimony. Just telling the judge yourself what you think is not enough. You need to get other people to come in and talk about the situation. If there is any evidence, such as documents or photos you can present, you need to bring those as well. You have the opportunity to cross-examine (ask questions of) anyone that testifies on behalf of your child's other parent.

The court will then make a decision based on what it thinks is best for your child. If you don't agree, you can appeal; however, an appeal only looks at whether the judge applied the law correctly and usually does not reconsider the evidence. Should things in your situation change, you can always go back to court to try to get the order altered to reflect the new circumstances.

Child Support

Each state has clear child support laws that are applied by family court when parents cannot agree. You can find your state child support laws online at *www.supportguidelines.com/links.html*. Basically, child support is calculated as a percent of the noncustodial parent's income (although the actual process used by the court involves a comparison using both parents' incomes). See Chapter 2 for exact percentages.

Although these are the standard guidelines, it is possible to opt out of them if you both agree and the hearing examiner agrees. Child support hearings are fairly routine and require the parents to disclose their income and assets. You usually have the choice of having payments sent directly to the parent receiving them or having payment go through the state child support office. The child support office can automatically enforce for nonpayment, which can be easier. Child support can be modified if there is a change in circumstances or income.

Spousal Support

There are no laws that require unmarried partners to support each other. If you want some kind of financial support after you break up, there is no standard legal process to request it, like there is for alimony. You can, as discussed earlier in this chapter, come to an agreement on your own without any help from the courts.

If you are unable to reach an agreement and believe you are entitled to support, something to consider is palimony. Palimony is court-ordered payments to a companion. It was first conceived in the 1970s in California. Most states now have palimony case law. Palimony is ordered by a court when the court determines that there was a real or implied contract between the partners to support one another, often when one partner stays home to care for the children. It sounds simple, but it can be hard to prove the existence of this kind of contract if you don't have anything in writing. To seek payments in a palimony case, you need an attorney who is experienced in this area of law.

Property Division

There are no laws specifically governing the division of property and debts between unmarried couples, but if you absolutely cannot agree, you can always go to small claims court, or if the amount of your dispute is over the small claims limit, you could head to the next court up the chain in your area (county or state court). The problem with this path of action is that these courts are not accustomed to resolving this kind of domestic matter. This normally falls into the jurisdiction of divorce court, but because there is no legal marriage, there is no other path available.

A court in this situation would seek to understand who contributed to the asset or debt and how it was managed during the course of the relationship. These cases are unreliable at best, and if at all possible, this is something to work out on your own.

Parenting Apart

If you and your partner break up, you transition from parenting your child simultaneously to parenting separately and at different times. While it can sometimes be a relief to be able to make parenting decisions on your own, it can also be challenging and emotionally difficult to do so.

Creating a Separate Parenting Relationship

Although you and your partner will need a lot of time to heal from your breakup, you must continue to be parents together. This requires you to make a kind of mental shift. You need to separate out in your mind your parenting relationship from your relationship as partners. Although you are no longer life partners, you are and will always be parents together, so you must find a way to work together with as little conflict as possible. It can be challenging to keep these two relationships separate, and of course there will be times when they bleed over into each other, but the more separate you can keep it, the more successful you will be. For example, while it might give you great personal satisfaction to pick up your child two hours late, because you know it will throw a wrench into your ex's plans with his or her new romantic interest, playing games with your child causes your child distress and makes it very difficult to work calmly and rationally with your ex. Also, this kind of behavior will damage your relationship with your child.

Advocacy Tip ▬▬▬▬▬▬▬▬▬▬▬▬▬▬▬▬▬

Parents Without Partners *www.parentswithoutpartners.org* is an international organization that is grassroots oriented. The heart of the organization is the local chapters, where parents can meet other parents. They often have family activities so children can get to know kids like them. At the national level, the organization works hard at advocating for single parents. This is an excellent opportunity to become involved and shape policy that affects single parents.

Business Transaction Approach

There are times when being civil to your ex might feel nearly impossible, and there are some relationships that are high conflict and volatile no matter what you do. In these situations, the best approach is to take what we call the business transaction approach. Instead of allowing yourself to get caught up in your ex's emotional vortex or letting your anger take over the situation, approach your parenting transactions (handing off your child, making schedules, negotiating changes) in a dry, businesslike manner. If you were in a meeting with a difficult client, you would hold your emotions in check so that you could complete the transaction. You need to learn to do the same thing when dealing with your ex if a more cooperative approach does not work.

Third-Party Assistance

Sometimes parents just cannot get along. Every time they see each other, they get into an argument. In such cases, a good solution is for one parent to leave the child with a third party, such as daycare, and the other parent to pick the child up from the daycare a half hour later. Sometimes relatives or friends can also take on this third-party role.

Helping Your Child after a Breakup

When you and your partner break up, it may not be technically called a divorce, but the impact is exactly the same. Your child's family configuration is changing. Even if you and your ex are committed to equal parenting time and cooperative parenting, this is still a major change for your child. It is essential you help your child understand he or she did not cause this or do anything that affected it. Children in these situations often blame themselves.

Understanding Your Child's Behavior

Some parents are surprised at the unpredictable behavior they see their child exhibiting. You might expect your child to cry, be angry, or express his or her emotions. Some children do, but others simply don't do so immediately. Each child reacts in his or her own individual way. Your role as a parent is to be there through the ups and downs with support, encouragement, and love. Some children hit a very rough patch months after the initial split. Some children find it harder to cope when they reach a certain age, such as the tween years. There is no set pathway your child will follow as he or she learns to live with the separation.

Taking Sides

It is common for children to take sides, and it is also common for children to be completely two-faced and side with the parent they are with, then switch sides as soon as they go to the other parent's home. Don't ever ask your child to take sides. This is one of the most important points to keep in mind. Asking your child to take sides is very dangerous to your child's mental and emotional health.

Do not discuss the details of the separation or the details of the reasons behind it. Those are adult details children do not need to focus on. Instead, direct your attention to trying to create a sense of normalcy for your child with a reliable schedule that is comfortable for everyone.

Disneyland Dad

The Disneyland Dad syndrome—where a nonresidential parent works in overdrive to make every second spent with the child fun, exciting, and fantastic—is to be avoided. Children need to simply live with both of their parents. They need to spend time at home—doing homework, washing dishes together, playing games, making popcorn, and so on. Doing something special once in a while is great, but it should not be the backbone of a parent-child relationship.

Children Are Not Go-Betweens

A common pitfall that separated parents make is using their child as a go-between. "Tell Daddy that his child support check is late." "Tell Mom we have to switch weekends." "Ask Dad if he thinks I am made of money." It might seem simple and convenient to ask your child to pass a message along, or even hand a check over, but involving your child in this way puts him or her smack in the middle of the conflict. Even though you do not intend to direct your anger or frustration at your child, you are in effect, asking him or her to carry it for you, present it to the other parent, and deal with the reaction. This is not fair to your child. Parents need to handle parenting arrangements themselves. Use the phone, e-mail, instant messenger or U.S. mail if you can't speak face to face.

Help for Your Child

It can be helpful to take your child to see a therapist who is experienced in working with children of divorce. There is an organization called Banana Splits that sponsors after-school meetings and activities for children of divorce. Middle school and high school guidance counselors also often hold lunch or after-school group sessions for children whose families are experiencing separation or divorce. These kinds of support groups can be very helpful for children, but many schools don't know about your divorce unless you tell them and ask them to help your child.

Life Lessons

A'isha and Ryan had lived together since their son Vaughn was born. Now, eight years later, they had come to the conclusion that their relationship was over. This was a painful decision, but one that had been many years in the making. Ryan was moving out into a condo he purchased, and A'isha was remaining in the home they had shared. A'isha had left her job as a bank teller when Vaughn was born, and now she wanted to go back to school to become a teacher. Ryan was continuing in his current job but hoped to one day open his own business.

Although A'isha and Ryan could certainly have some loud disagreements, they both felt that making sure Vaughn was okay through the change in their family needed to be their priority. They agreed he would spend two days a week at Ryan's house and five days at A'isha's. They agreed to a child support payment that met their state guidelines. They went to court and entered a stipulation for custody and child support so that everything was official. Vaughn had a therapist he saw for help with attention-deficit/hyperactivity disorder, and he continued to see her to help him through the separation process.

However, A'isha was in a difficult financial spot. She needed to go back to school, find a part-time job, make the mortgage payments on the house, and pay all the utility bills. She was really angry that there was no court mechanism for spousal support for her, even though she had lived with Ryan as a family for eight years. She and Ryan spent a lot of time arguing about their financial situation. She wanted him to pay her money every month, since she had stayed home with their child for so long. He resented being asked to pay her way.

Finally A'isha and Ryan went to see a mediator. With the mediator's help, they eventually agreed that Ryan would pay A'isha's tuition while she got her degree and teaching certificate. He would also give her an amount of money in cash every month that she could use to help manage her bills. That payment, coupled with the child support and her part-time job, allowed A'isha to support herself and her son.

Appendix A:
Sample Forms

Daycare Authorization

I, _____, parent of the child _____, authorize _____ to pick up my child from daycare at any time, without any advance notice by me.

_____   _____
Signed   *Dated*

School Authorization

I,_____, parent of the child_____, authorize _____ to attend all school functions, conferences, and events and to pick up my child at any time without any advance notice from me. I also authorize all teachers and school personnel to discuss my child and my child's progress or work with _____ at any time, as they would with me.

_____   _____
Signed   *Dated*

Consent to Obtain Medical Treatment

I, _____, parent of the child _____, DOB _____, authorize _____ to seek health care for my child in my absence without any further authorization from me.

_____   _____
Signed   *Dated*

Child Support Payment Tracking Worksheet

Date	Amount	Notes
_____	_____	_____
_____	_____	_____
_____	_____	_____
_____	_____	_____
_____	_____	_____
_____	_____	_____
_____	_____	_____
_____	_____	_____
_____	_____	_____

Voluntary Acknowledgment of Paternity Sample Form

To view a sample Voluntary Acknowledgement of Paternity form go to *www.co-childsupport.com/elpaso/forms/acknowledgement.pdf.* Section 1 lays out the legal effect of signing the document. The rest of the document asks for both parties to acknowledge paternity.

Sample Paternity Petition Form

To view a sample Paternity Petition form go to *www.courts.state.ny.us/forms/familycourt/pdfs/5-1.doc.* If you look at the document, you will see that in question number two the dates of sexual intercourse have to be listed. In number three you can see that that case can be brought before the child is born. In number six you can indicate the father's acknowledgment of paternity.

Appendix B:
Book and Web Resources

Book Resources

Cebuhar, Jo Kline. *Last Things First: The Practical Guide to Living Wills and Durable Powers of Attorney for Health Care.* West Des Moines, IA: Murphy, 2006.

Clifford, Dennis. *Make Your Own Living Trust.* Berkeley, CA: Nolo, 2007.

Engber, Andrea. *The Complete Single Mother: Reassuring Answers to Your Most Challenging Concerns.* Avon, MA: Adams Media, 2006.

Garrett, Sheryl. *Money Without Matrimony: The Unmarried Couple's Guide to Financial Security.* New York: Kaplan Business, 2005.

Gudgel, David. *Before You Live Together.* Ventura, CA: Regal Books, 2003.

Hoerner, Thomas. *The Ultimate Survival Guide for the Single Father.* Richmond, VA: Harbinger Press, 2002.

Ihara, Toni Lynne. *Living Together: A Legal Guide for Unmarried Couples.* Berkeley, CA: Nolo, 2006.

Mattes, Jane. *Single Mothers by Choice.* New York: Three Rivers Press, 1994.

Morrissette, Mikki. *Choosing Single Motherhood: The Thinking Woman's Choice.* Minneapolis, MN: Be-Mondo, 2006.

Noel, Brook. *The Single Parent Resource.* Beverly Hills, CA: Champion, 1998.

Solot, Dorian, and Marshall Miller. *Unmarried to Each Other: The Essential Guide to Living Together as an Unmarried Couple.* New York: Marlowe & Company, 2002.

Whitman, Stacey. *Shacking Up: The Smart Girl's Guide to Living in Sin Without Getting Burned.* New York: Broadway, 2003.

Wolfe, Leanna, *Women Who May Never Marry: The Reasons, Realities, and Opportunities.* Atlanta, GA: Longstreet Press, 1993.

Web Site Resources

Alternatives to Marriage Project
www.unmarried.org

American Association of Tissue Banks
www.aatb.org

American Society of Reproductive Medicine
www.asrm.org

Child Care Questionnaire Checklist
www.naccrra.org/docs/parent/38IndicatorsChecklist.pdf

Child Support Guidelines and Enforcement Units
www.supportguidelines.com/links.html

Employer Adoption Benefits
www.adoptionfriendlyworkplace.org

Family Medical Leave Act (FMLA)
www.dol.gov/esa/whd/fmla/

Family Equality Council
www.familyequality.org

Fertility Plus (sperm banks list and other donor resources)
www.fertilityplus.org/faq/donor.html

Insure Kids Now (health insurance through state plans)
www.InsureKidsNow.gov

National Adoption Foundation
www.nafadopt.org

National Endowment for Financial Education (information about affording adoption)
www.nefe.org/adoption/

Parents Without Partners
www.parentswithoutpartners.org

Pregnancy Discrimination Act
www.eeoc.gov/facts/fs-preg.html

Sample Home Study
www.1-800-homestudy.com/homestudy/sample

Single-Parent Support Sites
Making Lemonade *www.makinglemonade.com*
Single Rose *www.singlerose.com*
Single Parents Network *www.singleparentsnetwork.com*
Single Mothers by Choice *www.singlemothersbychoice.com*
Single Mothers *www.singlemothers.org*
Single Moms *www.singlemoms.com*
Solo Mother *www.solomother.com*

State Will Requirements
www.livingtrustnetwork.com/content/lwt/applicable_state_laws/
requirements_for_wills/index.php

Stepfamily Support Sites
Stepfamily Network *www.stepfamily.net*
National Stepfamily Resource Center *www.stepfamilies.info*
National Stepfamily Day *www.nationalstepfamilyday.com*
Stepparent Adoption Factsheet for Families *www.childwelfare.gov/pubs/*
f_step.cfm
Stepfamily Magazine *www.stepfamilymagazine.com*

U.S. Living Will Registry
www.USLivingWillRegistry.com

Index